CONTEMPORARY

INTRODUCTORY

reading

basics

A REAL-WORLD APPROACH TO LITERACY

McGraw Hill Education

Bothell, WA • Chicago, IL • Columbus, OH • New York, NY

Image Credits: Cover Lisa Fukshansky/The McGraw-Hill Companies

www.mheonline.com

 **Education**

Send all inquiries to:
Contemporary/McGraw-Hill
130 East Randolph Street, Suite 400
Chicago, IL 60601

ISBN: 978-0-07-659097-1
MHID: 0-07-659097-6

Printed in the United States of America.

4 5 6 7 8 9 QVS/QVS 18 17 16 15

Contents

UNIT 1

Lesson 1.1

Lesson 1.2

Lesson 1.3

Lesson 1.4

Lesson 1.5

Lesson 1.6

Lesson 1.7

UNIT 2

Lesson 2.1

Lesson 2.2

To the Student

Reading Basics will help you become a better reader. Research in evidence-based reading instruction (EBRI) has shown that reading has four important components, or parts: comprehension, alphabetics, vocabulary, and fluency. *Reading Basics* provides evidence-based reading instruction and practice in all four components. With your teacher's help, you can use the *Student Edition* and the articles in the *Introductory Reader* to gain important skills.

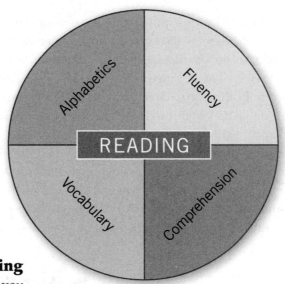

The Four Components of Reading

Comprehension *Reading Basics* teaches you many ways to improve your reading comprehension. Each lesson in the *Student Edition* introduces a different reading comprehension skill. You apply the skill to passages and to a workplace document. You also apply the skill to the articles in the *Reader*. Your teacher will help you use monitoring and fix-up reading strategies. You will learn ways to clarify your understanding of passages that are confusing to you. In addition, each article in the *Reader* begins with a before-reading strategy. At the end of the article, you will complete comprehension and critical thinking exercises.

Alphabetics In the *Student Edition* lessons, you will learn and practice alphabetics. Alphabetics includes phonics and word analysis skills, such as recognizing long and short vowels and syllable patterns, correctly spelling possessives and plurals, and studying word parts, such as prefixes, suffixes, and base words. You can use alphabetics skills to help you read and understand difficult words. For more practice, go to www.mhereadingbasics.com and use *PassKey*. This online program provides skills instruction and guided feedback.

Vocabulary Studying academic vocabulary will help you as a learner. Your teacher will present and explain five academic vocabulary words that you will need to understand as you read each *Student Edition* lesson. You will have a chance to practice these words along with other important vocabulary skills such as recognizing and using synonyms, antonyms, and context clues.

Your teacher will also present and explain vocabulary words important to your understanding of the articles in the *Reader*. As you read each article, notice that some words are defined in the margins. Use the definition and the context of each word to help you understand it.

Fluency Your teacher will present activities to help you with fluency—that is, reading smoothly, quickly, and accurately. You will practice fluency with the passages in the *Student Edition* and the articles in the *Reader*. You can also go to www.mhereadingbasics.com to download or play MP3 recordings of the articles. Listening to fluent reading will help you develop your own fluency skills.

How to Use This Book

The *Student Edition* consists of 19 lessons split among three units. These lessons help prepare you for questions on classroom tests and on important assessments. Each lesson is eight pages long and focuses on a particular reading comprehension skill.

Begin by taking the Pretest. Use the Answer Key to check your answers. Circle any wrong answers and use the Evaluation Chart to see which skills you need to practice.

Your teacher will guide your class through each lesson in the book. You will have chances to practice and apply skills on your own and in small groups. At the end of each unit, complete the Unit Review and Assessment. The Assessment will help you check your progress. Your teacher may want to discuss your answers with you.

After you complete the lessons in the book, you will take the Posttest on pages 189–198. The Evaluation Chart and Answer Key on pages 199–200 will help you see how well you have mastered the skills. To achieve mastery, you must answer 80 percent of the questions correctly.

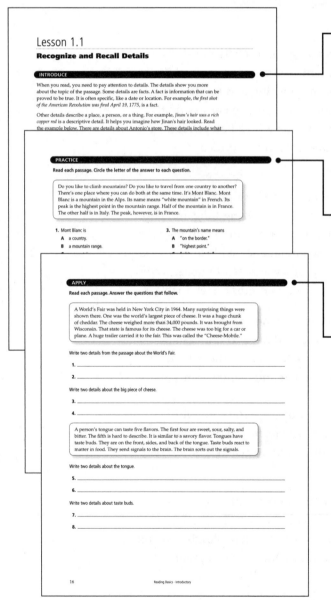

Working through Each Lesson

Introduce The first page of each lesson presents the reading skill. It also includes an example. Your teacher will use this example to explain and model the skill. Then your teacher will work with your class to do the guided practice at the bottom of the page. You will have a chance to practice this skill in the activities. Later in the lesson you will apply this skill to a document similar to one that you might use in the workplace.

Practice Next comes a page for practice. Usually, you will read a passage and answer questions about it that relate to the reading skill. You may be asked to fill out a graphic organizer to respond to a question. On some pages, there will be several passages followed by questions.

Apply The Apply page gives you a chance to apply the reading skill in a different way. In many lessons, you will read a passage and answer questions about it. You will see a variety of formats, including open-ended questions and graphic organizers.

Check Up The last page in the reading skills section of the lesson is the Check Up page. The questions on this page are always presented in a multiple-choice format. The Check Up page allows your teacher to monitor your progress as you learn the reading skill. Then your teacher can help you if you still have questions about the skill.

Workplace Skill The Workplace Skill page gives you another chance to practice the reading skill. Instead of using a reading passage, this page introduces the types of documents that you might find or need to use in the workplace. There could be a memo, a section of a handbook, or some kind of graph. You will read or study the document and answer questions about it.

The Workplace Skill documents relate to a wide variety of jobs. Some may be familiar to you, while others may be new.

Write for Work A Write for Work activity is at the top of the next page. You will do workplace-related writing such as drafting an e-mail or a memo. The writing relates to the document on the Workplace Skill page. This activity provides a chance for you to practice your writing skills and reading comprehension at the same time.

Reading Extension In most lessons, a Reading Extension comes next. Here you apply the reading skill to an article in the *Reader*. After reading the article, you will answer multiple-choice and open-ended questions.

Workplace Extension Some lessons have a Workplace Extension instead of a Reading Extension. The Workplace Extension addresses work-related issues. These might include preparing for an interview or dressing appropriately for work. You will read a scenario in which a person is faced with a work problem or issue. Then you will answer questions about how the person handled the situation or what he or she should do next.

For each unit, your teacher will hand out a Workplace Skill Activity sheet. You will work with a partner or in small groups to practice skills similar to those in the Workplace Extension. Many of these activities include role-playing so that you can practice realistic conversations about the workplace.

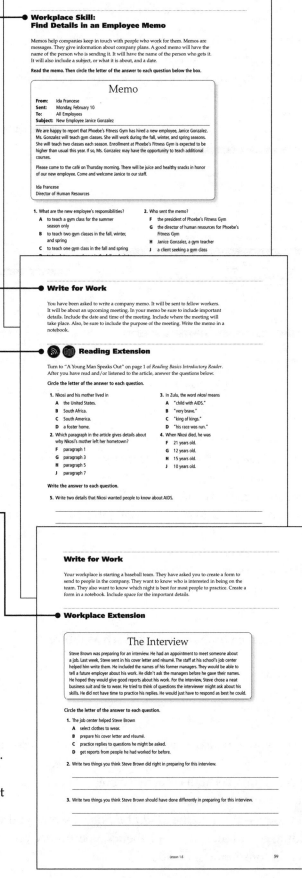

Explore Words You will practice two important reading skills in the Explore Words section of the lesson— alphabetics and vocabulary.

Each Explore Words section includes four or five activities. Each activity begins with brief instruction followed by practice. You may be asked to complete matching exercises, circle word parts, fill in missing words, or identify types of syllables.

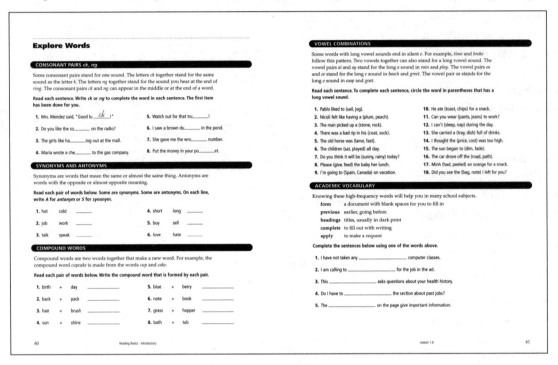

Here are some of the alphabetics skills that you will practice:
- short and long vowels
- vowel combinations and *r*-controlled vowels
- consonant blends and silent consonants
- hard and soft *c* and *g*
- possessives and contractions
- plurals and other word endings
- prefixes, suffixes, and base words
- syllable patterns

You will also practice vocabulary skills, such as these:
- context clues
- multiple-meaning words
- synonyms
- antonyms

In every lesson you will also work with the five academic vocabulary words your teacher will present before you begin reading the lesson. These words appear in context in the lesson. The Academic Vocabulary activity presents definitions of the words. You will use the words to complete sentences.

As you progress through the *Student Edition* lessons, you will notice improvements in your reading comprehension, alphabetics, vocabulary, and fluency skills. You will be a stronger and more confident reader.

Pretest

Read each passage. Then circle the letter of the answer to each question.

> Fleas are great jumpers. A flea can leap 13 inches in a single jump. That may not seem like much. However, fleas are only a fraction of an inch long. They can jump over 100 times their own length. If people could jump that far in relation to their size, they could jump about 600 feet. The longest human jump on record is just over 29 feet.

1. How far can a flea leap in a single jump?

    A   a fraction of an inch

    B   13 inches

    C   29 feet

    D   60 feet

2. What things are being compared and contrasted?

    F   leaping and jumping

    G   fleas and people

    H   inches and feet

    J   fleas and ticks

3. What is the best paraphrase of the first four sentences in the passage?

    A   Fleas are good jumpers. They can leap up to 13 inches even though they are very small.

    B   Even though it doesn't seem like much, a flea can jump really far.

    C   Fleas are great jumpers.

    D   Fleas measure 13 inches and can only jump a fraction of an inch at a time.

> Antlers and horns both grow on the heads of animals. They are not the same, though. In general, horns do not grow branches. They are attached to the animal's head by a bony core. They grow throughout the animal's life. Cows, goats, and sheep all have horns. Both males and females have them. Antlers have branches and are shed once a year. Antlers are more beautiful than horns. New antlers grow each year to replace the ones that are shed. Each set of antlers grows more branches than the last. Antlers usually grow only on male animals.

4. Which animal has antlers?

    F   sheep

    G   cows

    H   goats

    J   not stated

5. Which sentence is an opinion?

    A   In general, horns do not grow branches.

    B   Both males and females have them.

    C   Antlers are more beautiful than horns.

    D   They grow throughout the animal's life.

6. Horns grow

    F   for the first year.

    G   during the animal's adult life.

    H   during the entire life of the animal.

    J   into branched shapes.

7. What is one conclusion you can draw about antlers based on the passage?

    A   Antlers and horns are really the same thing.

    B   Females usually don't have antlers.

    C   Antlers never break.

    D   Animals have a difficult time growing antlers.

Pretest continued

Study the graph. Then circle the letter of the answer to each question.

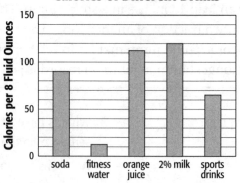

Calories of Different Drinks

Calories per 8 Fluid Ounces

Type of Drink

8. About how many fewer calories does soda have than 2% milk?

  F   10

  G   30

  H   60

  J   90

9. Which drink has the fewest calories?

  A   soda

  B   fitness water

  C   2% milk

  D   sports drinks

10. About how many calories does orange juice have?

  F   50

  G   80

  H   110

  J   130

11. Which drink has about 120 calories?

  A   soda

  B   orange juice

  C   2% milk

  D   sports drinks

Read the passage. Then circle the letter of the answer to each question.

> Owls cough up pellets after eating. The pellets often contain feathers, fur, scales, and bones. Scientists examine these pellets to learn about owls. They pull them apart to see just what the owl has been eating.

12. What causes scientists to pull apart owl pellets?

  F   They want to see what the owls have been eating.

  G   They want to retrieve bones.

  H   They want to find a better food for the owls.

  J   They want to find a way to stop owls from coughing up pellets.

13. What is the best summary of this passage?

  A   Owls eat a lot of random things.

  B   Scientists who study owls disect owl pellets to learn why owls eat things they can't digest.

  C   Scientists learn what owls have been eating by examining the pellets the owls cough up.

  D   Owls are messy eaters.

Read each passage. Then circle the letter of the answer to each question.

> Most languages develop over many, many years. There are a few, though, that specific people invented. They are called artificial languages. One of these languages is called Esperanto. A Polish man named L. L. Zamenhof created the language in the 1800s. Esperanto is derived from European languages. Zamenhof used these languages as a base, but he tried to make his language simpler. After his book about the language came out, some people began learning it. Today, there are more than 100,000 Esperanto speakers and more than 30,000 books published in the language. It is the most successful of all the artificial languages.

14. As used in the passage, what does the phrase *is derived from* mean?

   F is based on

   G is completely different from

   H is exactly the same as

   J is contained in

15. What is the main idea of this passage?

   A Over 100,000 people speak Esperanto even though it is an artificial language.

   B L. L. Zamenhof created Esperanto, which is the most popular of the artificial languages.

   C Many people learn Esperanto even though there is no need.

   D L. L. Zamenhof created the most popular language in the world.

> Some people think the best way to make foods last is to freeze them. Other people store foods in cans. There is another, older way to keep food from spoiling. Native Americans used heat from the sun to preserve food. They hung meat in the sun to dry it out. When the moisture is gone, germs can't grow and spread. Germs need water to stay alive. Today, most people don't hang meat in the sun. They often keep foods in moisture-proof packages.

16. Because foods are dried,

   F they spoil more quickly.

   G they are easier to freeze.

   H they lack the moisture that allows germs to live.

   J they are stored in cans.

17. What do you think the author's purpose was for writing this passage?

   A to entertain with a story about food preservation

   B to explain why drying foods keeps them from spoiling

   C to persuade readers to learn food-drying techniques

   D to describe Native American culture

Pretest continued

Circle the letter of the answer that gives the meaning of each sign.

18.

- **F** railroad crossing
- **G** bus stop
- **H** reserved for disabled persons
- **J** no U-turn

19.

- **A** do not enter
- **B** stop
- **C** no left turn
- **D** deer crossing

20.

- **F** stop
- **G** walk
- **H** merge
- **J** yield

21.

- **A** bicycle route
- **B** signal ahead
- **C** divided highway
- **D** no left turn

Read the passage. Then circle the letter of the answer to each question.

Alonzo and Kasim sat on the bench. They laced up their shoes. Kasim watched Alonzo from the corner of his eye.

"How do you feel?" Kasim asked.

Alonzo shrugged his shoulders. He stood up and stretched his leg on the bench.

Kasim finished tying his shoes. He couldn't wait to start running. He'd been training every morning. He'd been trying to get in shape and improve his time. His legs felt full of energy. He started bouncing up and down.

Alonzo finished stretching. "Let's go."

Kasim lined up at the starting line. He'd lost to Alonzo every time they'd raced, but this time, it would be different. His training had to pay off. He couldn't lose.

22. How do you predict Kasim will feel if he loses?

- **F** happy
- **G** disappointed
- **H** content
- **J** greedy

23. Name one character trait of Kasim's.

- **A** lazy
- **B** competitive
- **C** humorous
- **D** supportive

Pretest continued

Study the map. Then circle the letter of the answer to each question.

SOUTH RIDGE MALL

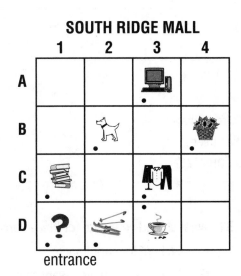

entrance

Key

24. What is located at coordinate D2?

    F   Ski Chalet

    G   Information Booth

    H   Pete's Pet Shop

    J   Computer Central

25. Where is Classic Books located?

    A   A3

    B   B2

    C   C1

    D   D3

26. What is located at coordinate A3?

    F   A1 Cleaners

    G   Computer Central

    H   Pete's Pet Shop

    J   Gardeners' Grove

27. Where is A1 Cleaners located?

    A   A1

    B   B2

    C   C1

    D   C3

28. How far is it from The Coffee Cafe to Computer Central?

    F   about 50 yards

    G   about 100 yards

    H   about 150 yards

    J   about 500 yards

29. What does the symbol stand for?

    A   A1 Cleaners

    B   Gardeners' Grove

    C   The Coffee Cafe

    D   Classic Books

Pretest continued

Read the warranty card that came with a recently purchased dishwasher. Then circle the letter of the answer to each question.

Warranty Card

Serial No. _____   Color _____

Model _____

Name _____   Mail to:

Address _____   KitchenStore Appliances

Date of Purchase _____   2434 Main Street

Place Purchased _____   Columbus, OH 43212

---

30. What should you write for Date of Purchase?

   F today's date

   G the date you bought the item

   H the date you plan to mail the item in

   J nothing

31. What should you do after you fill out this form?

   A file it in your file cabinet

   B call KitchenStore customer service

   C take it to the store where you bought the appliance

   D mail it to KitchenStore Appliances

32. What should you write for Place Purchased?

   F KitchenStore Appliances

   G the place where you want to pick up a replacement

   H the place where you bought the appliance

   J your home address

33. What does *Serial No.* mean?

   A serial number

   B this is not part of a series

   C serial north

   D serial negative

Read the dictionary entry. Then circle the letter of the answer to each question.

---

shine (shīn) *v.* **1.** to emit rays of light; **2.** to glow or be bright with reflected light; **3.** to be brilliant or outstanding at something; **4.** to make an object bright by rubbing or polishing it

---

34. Which set of guide words would be on the page on which *shine* is located?

   F shoot, shut

   G sample, sharp

   H shape, shingle

   J shingle, shore

35. Which meaning of *shine* is used in the following sentence?

When Winona dances, she really shines.

   A 1

   B 2

   C 3

   D 4

Pretest continued

Read the workplace document. Then circle the letter of the answer to each question.

You must count the money in your drawer when you finish your shift. First, print out a register report. Log in to your register and press *report*. The register report will print on receipt paper.

Each drawer starts with a base of $150 cash. When you count out, leave that amount in your drawer. We prefer these amounts:

- two rolls of pennies ($0.50 each)
- one roll of nickels ($2.00)
- one roll of dimes ($5.00)
- one roll of quarters ($10.00)

- 52 ones
- 10 fives
- 3 tens

It is best not to include twenties or bills of a higher value.

Next count the cash remaining. It should match the *cash* line on your printout. If the values do not match, you have a discrepancy. Recount your drawer and cash. Notify a manager if you still have a discrepancy—over or under—of $0.25 or more.

Then add the values of all checks in your drawer. Notify a manager if the total does not match the *checks* line on your printout.

Next, place the cash and checks in a zippered deposit bag. A manager will place your drawer and deposit in the safe. The entire process should take about 10 minutes. It is easy after you get some practice. You will be paid for this time.

36. What happens after you place your excess cash and checks in a deposit bag?

  F You should count your checks.

  G You print a register report.

  H A manager places the drawer and deposit in the safe.

  J You count the base of $150 into your drawer.

37. According to the instructions, what is one way in which counting cash and adding checks are similar?

  A You should count them each twice

  B You should notify a manager if there is a discrepancy.

  C The drawer should start with $150 in cash and $150 in checks.

  D You should place the cash in the zippered bag and return checks to the drawer.

38. Which sentence is an opinion?

  F You must count your drawer when you finish your shift.

  G Each drawer starts with a base of $150 cash.

  H The register report will print on receipt paper.

  J It is easy after you get some practice.

39. What does the word *discrepancy* mean?

  A good thing

  B difference

  C cash value

  D exact match

Pretest continued

Read the workplace document. Then circle the letter of the answer to each question.

Cake and Cupcake Order Form

Name _____   Date cake is needed _____

Phone _____   Circle one: delivery / pickup

Credit card _____

Expiration/CVV _____ / _____

Size (check one)
- ☐ 8-inch round
- ☐ 9-inch round
- ☐ half sheet (16" × 12")
- ☐ full sheet (24" × 16")
- ☐ cupcakes (one dozen)

Cake flavors (check one)
- ☐ carrot
- ☐ chocolate
- ☐ lemon
- ☐ red velvet
- ☐ strawberry
- ☐ yellow

Frosting flavors (check one)
- ☐ chocolate
- ☐ whipped cream
- ☐ butter cream
- ☐ cream cheese

Fillings (cakes only)
- ☐ lemon
- ☐ raspberries and cream
- ☐ white chocolate mousse

Special instructions

_____

_____

---

40. What fillings are available for cupcakes?

  F lemon

  G raspberries and cream

  H white chocolate mousse

  J No fillings are available.

41. If the customer is ordering a cake for a surprise birthday party and doesn't want calls at home, where should this information be written?

  A under special instructions

  B on the date cake is needed line

  C on the credit card line

  D in the side margin of the page

42. You are filling out the form for a customer, and you accidentally write today's date instead of the date the cake is needed. What do you predict will happen?

  F The cake will be ready on the date it is needed.

  G The order will be marked as filled.

  H You will have to try to remember what the customer wanted.

  J Someone will call the customer to find out when the cake is needed.

43. Which of these is NOT a frosting flavor?

  A lemon

  B chocolate

  C cream cheese

  D whipped cream

Pretest continued

Circle the letter of the answer to each question.

44. Which word has a short vowel sound?

   F   band

   G   cane

   H   foam

   J   hair

45. Which word has a soft *c* sound?

   A   coin

   B   clam

   C   cent

   D   cube

46. Which word means the opposite of the underlined word?

safe place

   F   harmless

   G   lively

   H   polished

   J   dangerous

47. Which phrase means "the bags belonging to several sisters"?

   A   the sister's bags

   B   the sisters bag

   C   the sister' bags

   D   the sisters' bags

48. Which word is the plural of *match*?

   F   matchs

   G   matches

   H   matechs

   J   matchis

49. Which two words are homophones?

   A   ring, rung

   B   book, broke

   C   care, chair

   D   pore, pour

50. Which word does not have the long *o* sound?

   F   broke

   G   groan

   H   home

   J   clot

51. Which word fits into both sentences?

Please _____ to see if the cake is done baking.

Farran wrote a _____ to his landlord for the rent.

   A   receipt

   B   look

   C   check

   D   item

52. Which is the correct meaning of *preview*?

   F   view incorrectly

   G   view before

   H   view under

   J   view without

53. Which word has a silent consonant?

   A   scrap

   B   hang

   C   barn

   D   wring

54. Which word means the same or about the same as the underlined word?

angry person

   F   mad

   G   happy

   H   sickly

   J   disgusting

55. In which word does *y* stand for the long *i* sound?

   A   happily

   B   apply

   C   simply

   D   pretty

56. Which word means "the most lovely"?

   F   loveliest

   G   lovelier

   H   lovelyest

   J   lovelyer

57. Which word means "to do again"?

   A   undo

   B   redo

   C   misdo

   D   predo

58. Which word is a compound word?

   F   unleash

   G   chipper

   H   pancake

   J   leading

59. Which word fits into both sentences?

Nizhoni wrapped the birthday _____ before he gave it to his friend.

At the _____ time, the company has no plans to expand.

   A   gift

   B   current

   C   present

   D   now

60. Which word correctly completes the sentence?

Minh couldn't figure out what to do and felt _____.

   F   purposeless

   G   mispurposed

   H   repurposed

   J   purposeful

61. In which word does *y* stand for the long *e* sound?

   A   rely

   B   cherry

   C   fry

   D   reply

62. Which word has an *r*-controlled vowel?

   F   scrap

   G   chart

   H   crown

   J   real

63. Which phrase means "the pages that belong to Neema"?

   A   Neema's pages

   B   Neemas' pages

   C   Neema's page

   D   Neemas' page

64. Which is the base word in the word *uncaring*?

   F   uncare

   G   caring

   H   uncar

   J   care

65. What is the meaning of *misread*?

   A   undo reading

   B   read without

   C   read again

   D   read incorrectly

66. In which word does *qu* stand for the *k* sound?

   F   bouquet

   G   quest

   H   sequel

   J   acquire

67. Which word is a contraction of *we are*?

   A   we're

   B   were

   C   wer'e

   D   wea're

This pretest was designed to help you determine which reading skills you need to study. This chart shows which skill is being covered with each test question. Use the key on page 12 to check your answers. Then circle the questions you answered incorrectly and go to the practice pages in this book covering those skills.

Tested Skills	Question Numbers	Practice Pages
Recognize and Recall Details	1, 6, 43	14–17
Understand Stated Concepts	4, 40	22–25
Draw Conclusions	7, 31	30–33
Summarize and Paraphrase	3, 13	38–41
Recognize Character Traits	23	46–49
Use Forms	30–33, 40–43	54–57
Use Correct Spelling	47, 48, 49, 56, 63, 67	21, 29, 44, 45, 62–65, 85, 93, 100, 117, 125, 148, 165, 172, 173, 180
Find the Main Idea	15	78–81
Identify Cause and Effect	12, 16	86–89
Use Consumer Materials	30–33	94–97
Identify Fact and Opinion	5, 38	102–105
Predict Outcomes	22, 42	110–113
Read Maps	24–29	118–121
Identify Sequence	31, 36	134–137
Compare and Contrast	2, 37	142–145
Identify Author's Purpose	17	150–153
Use Graphs	8–11	158–161
Read Signs	18–21	166–169
Use a Dictionary	34, 35	174–177
Synonyms/Antonyms	46, 54	20, 29, 60, 84, 116, 124, 141
Context Clues	14, 39, 51, 59, 60	37, 53, 69, 108, 140, 181
Phonics/Word Analysis	44, 45, 50, 52, 53, 55, 57, 58, 60, 61, 62, 64, 65, 66	20, 28, 36, 44, 52, 60, 61, 68, 84, 92, 100, 101, 108, 109, 116, 124, 140, 148, 149, 156, 157, 164, 172, 180

	KEY		
1.	B	36.	H
2.	G	37.	B
3.	A	38.	J
4.	J	39.	B
5.	C	40.	J
6.	H	41.	A
7.	B	42.	J
8.	G	43.	A
9.	B	44.	F
10.	H	45.	C
11.	C	46.	J
12.	F	47.	D
13.	C	48.	G
14.	F	49.	D
15.	B	50.	J
16.	H	51.	C
17.	B	52.	G
18.	F	53.	D
19.	C	54.	F
20.	H	55.	B
21.	A	56.	F
22.	G	57.	B
23.	B	58.	H
24.	F	59.	C
25.	C	60.	F
26.	G	61.	B
27.	D	62.	G
28.	G	63.	A
29.	B	64.	J
30.	G	65.	D
31.	D	66.	F
32.	H	67.	A
33.	A		
34.	H		
35.	C		

Unit 1

In this unit you will learn how to

You will practice the following workplace skills

You will also learn new words and their meanings and put your reading skills to work in written activities. You will get additional reading practice in *Reading Basics Introductory Reader*.

Lesson 1.1

Recognize and Recall Details

When you read, you need to pay attention to details. The details show you more about the topic of the passage. Some details are facts. A fact is information that can be proved to be true. It is often specific, like a date or location. An example of a fact is *the first shot of the American Revolution was fired April 19, 1775.*

Other details describe a place, a person, or a thing. For example, *Jinan's hair was a rich copper red* is a detail. It helps you imagine how Jinan's hair looked. Read the example below. It includes details about Antonio's store. The passage lists what he sells. It also includes how people feel about the store.

> Antonio owns a small grocery store. In the store, he sells food items. He sells bread, cheese, and milk. He also sells greeting cards. He takes pride in his store. Many people like to shop there. The customers enjoy talking to Antonio. He always smiles while he is working.

The details about Antonio's store are facts. You can prove that he owns a store. Do you want to know what Antonio sells in his store? The details in this example show you that he sells bread, cheese, and milk. The other details describe Antonio and his customers. Read the example below. It has details that are mainly description.

> The stone wall stood in the green pasture. The wall was old. It was made of uneven stones stacked on top of one another. Out in the far end of the pasture, cows dotted the landscape. Their brown and white spots stood out among the endless green grass.

Try to recognize and recall details. Then you will better understand and enjoy what you read.

This passage gives facts about tide pools at the seashore. Circle the names of two sea animals that live in tide pools.

> There is plenty of life on the seashore. Ocean water collects in little pools among the rocks. These are sometimes called tide pools. The pools are safe from waves. They are warmer than the ocean. Sea animals live in the pools. Hermit crabs live there. They live in the old shells of other animals. There are many empty shells in the pools. Starfish live there, too. They do well in the calm water.

Did you circle *hermit crabs* and *starfish*? These details name two sea animals that live in tide pools.

Read each passage. Circle the letter of the answer to each question.

Do you like to climb mountains? Do you like to travel from one country to another? There's one place where you can do both at the same time. It's Mont Blanc. Mont Blanc is a mountain in the Alps. Its name means "white mountain" in French. Its peak is the highest point in the mountain range. Half of the mountain is in France. The other half is in Italy. The peak, however, is in France.

1. Mont Blanc is

  A a country.

  B a mountain range.

  C a mountain.

  D a glacier.

2. Mont Blanc is in both

  F England and France.

  G France and Switzerland.

  H Spain and Italy.

  J France and Italy.

3. The mountain's name means

  A "on the border."

  B "highest point."

  C "white mountain."

  D "two countries."

4. From what language does Mont Blanc's name come?

  F English

  G French

  H Italian

  J Spanish

The largest land animals on Earth are African elephants. A male African elephant can weigh as much as 6 tons, or 12,000 pounds. Females are usually smaller than males. Both male and female African elephants have ivory tusks. The tusks are up to eight feet long. In the past, millions of African elephants were killed for their tusks. People used the ivory to make jewelry and other carved items. The elephants and their tusks are now protected. However, illegal killing is still a problem.

5. Female African elephants

  A have longer tusks than males.

  B weigh the same as males.

  C are usually smaller than males.

  D are usually larger than males.

6. An African elephant's tusks are

  F made of ivory.

  G turned into ivory.

  H not valuable.

  J thrown away.

7. How many African elephants were killed in the past?

  A a few

  B thousands

  C hundreds

  D millions

8. Ivory is used

  F for food.

  G to make jewelry.

  H to protect elephants.

  J to make tusks.

Read each passage. Then answer the questions.

> The World's Fair of 1964 was held in New York City. Many surprising things were shown there. One was the world's largest piece of cheese. It was a huge chunk of cheddar. The cheese weighed more than 34,000 pounds. It was brought from Wisconsin. That state is famous for its cheese. The cheese was too big for a car or plane. A huge trailer carried it to the fair. It was called the "Cheese-Mobile."

Write two details from the passage about the World's Fair.

1. _____

2. _____

Write two details about the big piece of cheese.

3. _____

4. _____

> A person's tongue can taste five flavors. The first four are sweet, sour, salty, and bitter. The fifth is hard to describe. It is similar to a savory flavor. Tongues have taste buds. They are on the front, sides, and back of the tongue. Taste buds react to matter in food. They send signals to the brain. The brain sorts out the signals.

Write two details about the tongue.

5. _____

6. _____

Write two details about taste buds.

7. _____

8. _____

Read each passage. Then circle the letter of the answer to each question.

> In villages in India, some people live in mud houses. These people are very poor. They cannot build any other kind of house. Mud is free. The people take wet mud and make blocks. They dry these mud blocks in the sun. Dried mud is very strong. The people tie the blocks together with straw and build their homes with them. In some villages, all the buildings are made of mud blocks.

1. In what country do people use mud blocks to build houses?

  A United States

  B India

  C Israel

  D Ireland

2. What is the main reason mud blocks are used?

  F Mud looks nice.

  G Mud keeps houses warm.

  H Mud is easy to build with.

  J Mud is free.

3. What material is used to tie mud blocks together?

  A straw

  B wood

  C clay

  D cement

4. How do people dry mud blocks?

  F in the rain

  G in the sun

  H in a well

  J in an oven

> Today, grocery store freezers are filled with frozen foods. We have frozen foods because of a man named Clarence Birdseye. He saw that people in the Arctic froze fish and meat for later use. Birdseye thought he could do the same thing. He packed fresh fish and meat in wax boxes. Then he used ice, salt water, and an electric fan to quickly freeze them. Birdseye first sold frozen fish in 1925. Many of the frozen foods in your grocery store today have the name Birds Eye.

5. What is Clarence Birdseye best known for?

  A freezing food

  B exploring the Arctic

  C catching fish

  D inventing the electric fan

6. What kind of food did people in the Artic freeze?

  F desserts

  G fruit

  H vegetables

  J meat and fish

7. Birdseye first froze food

  A in his own freezer.

  B with ice, salt water, and a fan.

  C in 1940.

  D in 1950.

8. One popular brand of frozen foods today is

  F Artic Meats.

  G Clarence Foods.

  H Birds Eye.

  J Iced Foods.

Workplace Skill: Find Details in an Employee Memo

Memos are messages. They are often in the form of an e-mail. A good memo shows the name of the person who is sending it. It shows the name of the person who gets it. It also shows the subject of the memo, or what it is about, and a date.

People who work in companies use memos often. A memo can let people know the time of a meeting. A memo can include details about an event. Someone might use a memo to let others know what they need to do next.

Read the memo. Then circle the letter of the answer to each question below the box.

Memo

From: Ida Francese
Sent: Monday, February 10
To: All Employees
Subject: New Employee Janice Gonzalez

We are happy to report that Phoebe's Fitness Gym has hired a new employee, Janice Gonzalez. Ms. Gonzalez will teach gym classes. She will work during the fall, winter, and spring seasons. She will teach two classes each season. Enrollment at Phoebe's Fitness Gym is expected to be higher than usual this year. If so, Ms. Gonzalez may have the opportunity to teach additional courses.

Please come to the café on Thursday morning. There will be juice and healthy snacks in honor of our new employee. Come and welcome Janice to our staff.

Ida Francese
Director of Human Resources
Phoebe's Fitness Gym

---

1. What are the new employee's responsibilities?

   A to teach a gym class for the summer season only

   B to teach two gym classes in the fall, winter, and spring

   C to teach one gym class in the fall and spring

   D to teach two gym classes in the fall and winter

2. Who sent the memo?

   F the president of Phoebe's Fitness Gym

   G the director of human resources for Phoebe's Fitness Gym

   H Janice Gonzalez, a gym teacher

   J a client seeking a gym class

Write for Work

You have been asked to write a company memo. It will be sent to fellow workers. It will be about an upcoming meeting. In your memo be sure to include important details. Include the date and time of the meeting. Include where the meeting will take place. Also, be sure to include the purpose of the meeting. Write the memo in a notebook.

  # Reading Extension

Turn to "A Young Man Speaks Out" on page 1 of *Reading Basics Introductory Reader*. After you have read and/or listened to the article, answer the questions below.

Circle the letter of the answer to each question.

1. Nkosi and his mother lived in
   - **A** the United States.
   - **B** South Africa.
   - **C** South America.
   - **D** a foster home.

2. Which paragraph in the article gives details about why Nkosi's mother left her hometown?
   - **F** paragraph 1
   - **G** paragraph 3
   - **H** paragraph 5
   - **J** paragraph 7

3. In Zulu, the word *nkosi* means
   - **A** "child with AIDS."
   - **B** "very brave."
   - **C** "king of kings."
   - **D** "his race was run."

4. When Nkosi died, he was
   - **F** 21 years old.
   - **G** 12 years old.
   - **H** 15 years old.
   - **J** 10 years old.

Write the answer to each question.

5. Write two details that Nkosi wanted people to know about AIDS.

_____

_____

6. Write two details that show how Nkosi was brave.

_____

_____

Explore Words

SHORT VOWELS

The letters *a, e, i, o,* and *u* are vowels. Every vowel has two sounds. You can hear the long vowel sounds in these words: *safe, Pete, mile, bone,* and *use.* You can hear the short vowel sounds in these words: *bad, beg, fit, box,* and *rug.*

Read each sentence. To complete each sentence, circle the word in parentheses that has a short vowel sound.

1. (Jen, Gene) has a good job.
2. Chenda sat on her mom's (cape, lap).
3. Suri got a new (bike, wig).

4. Ricardo (dropped, broke) the glass.
5. The king will (rule, run) the country.
6. I saw the kids (skip, hike) up the path.

CONSONANT BLENDS

The consonants *s, l, r,* and *n* can blend with other consonants. A consonant blend can come at the beginning of words. For example, read these words: *stop, grin,* and *skip.* A consonant blend can also come at the end of words. For example, read these words: *last* and *bank.* When you see a consonant blend, say the sounds of both consonants.

Read the sentences below. Complete each word with one of the consonant blends in parentheses. Make sure the word fits the meaning of the sentence. The first item has been done for you.

1. Salima has a new _____*bl*_____ue dress. **(bl, sl, gr)**

2. Hazel is _____ad to be in school. **(br, gl, st)**

3. Marco's oldest child is in first _____ade. **(bl, sl, gr)**

4. The baby has to _____ink a lot of milk. **(pr, sl, dr)**

5. He went to put money in the ba_____. **(sk, nk, st)**

6. Chaytan finished la_____ in the race. **(sk, nk, st)**

7. Yesterday is in the pa_____ . **(sk, nk, st)**

8. A sku_____ smells really bad. **(sk, nk, st)**

SYNONYMS

Synonyms are words that have the same or almost the same meaning. For example, *kind* and *nice* are synonyms.

Read each sentence. Circle the two words in each sentence that are synonyms.

1. Lomasi was sad. She was unhappy with her job.
2. Shing was a small baby. He is now a little boy.

3. Su shut the door. Then she closed a window.
4. Did you speak to Adiva? I will talk to her today.

SPELLING: POSSESSIVES

The words *Elian's car* show that the car belongs to Elian. Look at the *'s*. It is used to write possessive words. Possessive words show that something belongs to someone.

Read each phrase. Then use 's to write the possessive phrase. The first item has been done for you.

1. the son of Dara _____ *Dara's son* _____

2. the family of Farid _____

3. the book that belongs to the professor _____

4. the laptop that belongs to Grace _____

5. the hat that belongs to Tam _____

6. the birthday of Nuri _____

7. the car that belongs to my uncle _____

8. the mail that belongs to the neighbor _____

9. the notebook that belongs to Lise _____

10. the sweater that belongs to Yasir _____

ACADEMIC VOCABULARY

Knowing these high-frequency words will help you in many school subjects.

topic what a piece of writing is about

details facts that give information about a topic

recall to remember

describe to tell how something looks, sounds, tastes, smells, or feels

passage a short piece of writing

Complete the sentences below using one of the words above.

1. Can you _____ the date when we first met?

2. I read an interesting _____ about African elephants.

3. The police officer asked for _____ about the lost dog.

4. What is the _____ of your report?

5. It is hard to _____ what this tastes like.

Lesson 1.2

Understand Stated Concepts

There are concepts, or ideas, in every passage. Sometimes you have to put information together to understand ideas. Often, though, concepts and facts are stated directly. You can find them in the text. The text can state the meaning of new words. Make sure to pay attention to the stated concepts. When you can recognize directly stated ideas in the text, you will better understand what you read. Read the example below:

Polar bears live in the far north. A polar bear's thick fur helps to keep it warm.

The first sentence states where polar bears live. The second sentence shows how polar bears stay warm.

As you read, think about the meanings of words in bold print, titles, and headings. They may help you find information and understand what you are reading. Read the passage below. It states information about New Orleans and the Mississippi River.

The Crescent City

New Orleans is known as the Crescent City. The name comes from the shape of the Mississippi River. The city was built along a sharp bend in the river. It looked like a crescent moon. Today a bridge called the Crescent City Connection connects the east and west banks of the Mississippi.

A title helps you prepare for what you are about to read. This title states that you are going to read about something called the Crescent City. Next, the passage states that the Crescent City is New Orleans. It states that the name Crescent City comes from the crescent shape of the Mississippi River.

It is a good idea to take notes as you read. If you read a stated concept or fact that you want to remember, write it down or highlight it in some way. Taking notes will help you better understand and remember what you read.

Read the passage below. Underline the sentence that states the location of a rabbit's eyes.

(1) It is hard to sneak up behind a rabbit. (2) If you try, the rabbit will rush away. (3) It seems like it has eyes in the back of its head. (4) It doesn't. (5) It has the next best thing. (6) A rabbit's eyes are on the sides of its head. (7) Rabbits can see above and behind themselves. (8) They need good sight to spot hunters.

Did you underline sentence 6? It states, "A rabbit's eyes are on the sides of its head." This stated fact is important to understand and remember.

Read each passage. The read each question. If the answer is stated in the passage, circle *stated.* **If it is not stated, circle** *not stated.*

In Utah, there is a mountain where you can find fossils. Try tapping a rock open with a hammer. You might find the fossil of a large bug called a trilobite. It will probably be two or three inches long. This bug died around 500 million years ago. You can take the sheet of rock home. Just soak it in water. Then tap on the rock and the trilobite fossil will fall out.

1. Where can you find a trilobite?

    stated   not stated

2. How can you find a trilobite?

    stated   not stated

3. About how big is a trilobite?

    stated   not stated

4. What do people learn about animals from a trilobite?

    stated   not stated

5. Why would you soak a sheet of rock in water?

    stated   not stated

In Japan, the New Year is very important. People celebrate it for a whole week. They think the New Year is a time to make a fresh start. They clean their houses well. They pay old bills. They dress in their newest clothes. Children fly kites. People put branches on their doors. The branches send a wish for a long life.

6. How long do people celebrate the New Year in Japan?

    stated   not stated

7. Why is the New Year important in Japan?

    stated   not stated

8. How did the Japanese New Year customs begin?

    stated   not stated

9. How do Japanese people send their good wishes for others at the New Year?

    stated   not stated

10. How do people in other countries celebrate the New Year?

    stated   not stated

The largest group of fish are the bony fish. They have bony skeletons. Trout and many others belong to this group. All bony fish also have a tough outer covering of scales. Another group is the jawless fish. This group includes lampreys.

11. What is the largest group of fish?

    stated   not stated

12. To which group do smelt belong?

    stated   not stated

13. Which group of fish have scales?

    stated   not stated

14. How do jawless fish eat?

    stated   not stated

Read each passage. Then write an answer to each question. If the answer is not stated, write *not stated* on the line.

> The first movies did not have sound. They did not tell a story. They lasted only a few minutes, but many people went to see them. They showed a train going down a track. They showed people fighting. People were amazed to see moving pictures. One of the first movies with a story was shown in 1903. It was called *The Life of an American Fireman*.

1. Name two ways in which the first movies differed from those of today.

_____

2. Where did people go to see the earliest movies?

_____

3. What is the title of one of the first movies with a story?

_____

> At one time, no one threw passes in football games. Players either ran with the ball or kicked it. In a game in 1876, a runner got tackled. Then he threw the ball. It was a surprise. Passing in football became legal in 1906. Teams did not start to use passing plays right away.
>
> Knute Rockne was a football player famous for catching passes. In 1913 he played for the University of Notre Dame. Rockne caught many passes. The other teams were puzzled by Notre Dame's passing. Soon all the teams started passing the ball.

4. How did passing in football games begin in the 1800s?

_____

5. Who was the first football player famous for a passing game?

_____

6. Why did early teams not pass the ball?

_____

Read each passage. Then circle the letter of the answer to each question.

During the Ice Age, horses roamed North America. There were also horses in Asia and Europe. After the Ice Age, no horses were left in North America. Where did they go? Some say they all got sick and died. Other people think they were eaten by wild animals. These ideas do not seem right. Bison also lived in North America back then, but they were not killed. Bison lived through the Ice Age. No one knows why the horses died. There were no horses in the Americas until the Spanish brought them from Europe in the 1500s.

1. Where did horses live during the Ice Age?

  A only in Asia and Europe

  B only in North America

  C in North America, Asia, and Europe

  D nowhere

2. The passage talks about bison because

  F they didn't disappear when horses did.

  G they may have killed the horses.

  H they disappeared when the horses did.

  J they did not live in Europe.

3. What is one idea about why the North American horses disappeared?

  A They froze to death.

  B They went to Europe.

  C They were replaced by bison.

  D They got sick and died.

4. How did horses return to North America?

  F They got over their sickness.

  G They ate other animals.

  H They were brought by the Spanish from Europe.

  J No one knows.

The sport of rock climbing started in the 1800s. Rock climbing uses special equipment, such as ropes, harnesses, special shoes, and helmets. It also requires training. Some learners practice climbing in indoor gyms. They gain the skills and strength that they need. When they are ready, they climb on real rocks. Rock climbing is a fun sport, but it can be dangerous. The higher and steeper a climb, the more dangerous it is. Unless climbers are very close to the ground, they usually work in teams of two. Each climber has different tasks that keep the other one safe.

5. When did the sport of rock climbing start?

  A in the 1700s

  B in the 1800s

  C in the 1900s

  D in the 2000s

6. According to the passage, the sport of rock climbing is

  F completely safe.

  G fun but dangerous.

  H too dangerous to try.

  J easy to do without training.

Workplace Skill:
Identify Stated Concepts
in a Procedural Document

Procedural documents are common in the workplace. They tell you how to do something. Sometimes, the important ideas in a procedure are stated directly. Sometimes you have to figure them out.

Read the copy-room procedures document. Then circle the letter of the answer to each question below the box.

Copy-room Procedures

Please follow all copy-room procedures. These procedures will help keep the copiers in good working order. The copy room contains two copiers. One is for black-and-white copies. The other is for color copies. Do not use the color copier for black-and-white copies.

Both copiers work in the same way. Lift the lid of the copier. Place paper print side down, or place multiple papers in the top tray. Type in your copy code. This code keeps track of all the copies you make. Choose the number of copies. Press the green button. The copier will start copying. A yellow light appears if the copier is out of paper. Please refill the paper tray. Use copy paper only. If a red light appears, please call the copy service number. The number is posted above the copier. Always leave the copy room neat. Recycle all unwanted copies. Do not leave paper on top of the copier.

1. Which important idea is stated directly in the first paragraph?

   A   Copy-room procedures help keep copiers in good working order.

   B   The black-and-white copier cannot be used for color copies.

   C   It costs more money to make color copies.

   D   The color copier can make all the copies you will need.

2. Which idea is stated directly in the second paragraph?

   F   The red light will appear whenever the copier is broken.

   G   Employees should recycle unwanted copies following company policy.

   H   Employees are given approval for 100 copies per month without authorization.

   J   You should only use copy paper to refill the paper tray.

Write the answer to the question.

3. What procedure should employees follow if they see a red light on the copier?

_____

Reading Basics · Introductory

Write for Work

Imagine you need to explain to a coworker how to use the microwave or other small appliance in the office lunchroom. Write the procedure in a notebook. First, state the procedure for using the appliance. Then list three rules for using the appliance.

 Reading Extension

Turn to "Alone across the Atlantic" on page 9 of *Reading Basics Introductory Reader*. After you have read and/or listened to the article, answer the questions below.

Circle the letter of the answer to each question.

1. How many miles do teams row in the Ward Evans Atlantic Rowing Challenge?
   - **A** about 3,000 miles
   - **B** about 350 miles
   - **C** about 1,000 miles
   - **D** not stated

2. According to the story, why did Andrew become afraid of the open sea?
   - **F** He saw a shark circling the boat.
   - **G** A big ship almost hit the boat.
   - **H** His fingers were tired from gripping the oars.
   - **J** not stated

3. According to the story, what did Debra realize on the eighth day at sea?
   - **A** She had to get Andrew off the boat.
   - **B** Their boat developed a leak.
   - **C** She and Andrew would win the race.
   - **D** not stated

Write the answer to each question.

4. What effect did the salt spray have on Debra?

   _____

   _____

5. Where did Debra land at the end of the race?

   _____

Explore Words

SHORT AND LONG VOWELS

Every vowel has a long and a short sound. These words have short vowel sounds: *flat*, *bet*, *is*, *cot*, and *cub*. These words have long vowel sounds: *make*, *tree*, *mine*, *hold*, and *tune*.

Read each sentence. Then identify the vowel sound in the underlined word. Write *short* on the line if the vowel sound in the word is short. Write *long* if the vowel sound in the word is long.

1. Most people <u>like</u> to get free gifts. _____

2. It is important to <u>save</u> money. _____

3. Mr. Carlson <u>smiled</u> at Violet. _____

4. The tickets were a <u>fun</u> gift. _____

5. Julio <u>chose</u> the tickets. _____

6. The tickets were for a <u>play</u>. _____

7. Don't <u>miss</u> the first act! _____

8. You need to change a <u>fuse</u>. _____

CONSONANT PAIRS

Some consonant pairs stand for one sound. The letters *ch* together stand for the sound you hear at the beginning of *cheese* and at the end of *inch*. The letters *th* together stand for the sound you hear at the beginning of *thirst* and at the end of *bath*. The letters *th* can also stand for the sound you hear at the beginning of *then*.

Read each sentence. Then write *ch* or *th* to complete the word. Make sure the word fits the meaning of the sentence. The first item has been done for you.

1. I just love __*th*__ at scarf!

2. Marisa opened a bag of _____ips.

3. You have gotten very _____in.

4. Min is sitting on a ben_____.

5. My dog likes to _____ase the cat.

6. I walked to the store with _____em.

7. Can you rea_____ the top shelf?

8. Michele can _____ink for herself.

9. He will tea_____ his sisters to swim.

10. May I sit wi_____ you?

SPELLING: CONTRACTIONS

A **contraction** is a short way to write two words. The contraction *don't* is a shorter way to write the words *do not*. A contraction always has an apostrophe ('). It takes the place of the letters. In *don't,* the apostrophe takes the place of the letter *o* in *not*.

Read the contractions in the box. Then write each one next to its meaning.

wasn't	didn't	let's	it's

1. it is _____

2. was not _____

3. did not _____

4. let us _____

ANTONYMS

Antonyms are words with the opposite or almost opposite meanings. For example, the words *hot* and *cold* are antonyms.

Read each word in boldface type. Circle its antonym.

1. summer	December	winter	hot	cold
2. open	close	fasten	door	lock
3. short	fat	hard	tall	wide
4. start	begin	finish	grow	leak

ACADEMIC VOCABULARY

Knowing these high-frequency words will help you in many school subjects.

stated	said in speech or writing
concept	idea
directly	in a clear way
notes	written reminders
legal	allowed under the law

Complete the sentences below using one of the words above.

1. Don't speak in circles. Just tell me _____ where you have been.

2. Look over the _____ you took in class.

3. The recipe _____ that the oven should be set at 350°.

4. It isn't _____ to park in a crosswalk.

5. The boss came up with a new _____ for keeping track of our overtime.

Lesson 1.3

Draw Conclusions

Some facts and ideas are stated directly in a passage. Some ideas are not stated directly. If you think about what you read and what you already know, you can draw conclusions. Read the example below:

> The man read his son's report card. He frowned.

You can draw the conclusion that the man was unhappy with his son's grades. This makes sense. Frowning usually means someone is unhappy. You also know that report cards show grades. A conclusion that makes sense is a valid conclusion.

Suppose you draw a different conclusion. You think the man was happy with his son's grades. This does not make sense. The facts stated directly do not support this conclusion. What you know does not support this conclusion either. A conclusion that does not make sense is an invalid conclusion. Read the example below:

> On September 8, 1900, a hurricane struck the city of Galveston, Texas. The storm killed about 6,000 people. It was the deadliest natural disaster in U.S. history. Today, meteorologists track hurricanes with satellites and radar. They use computers to predict a storm's path. Their work allows people to prepare for a hurricane's arrival.

Suppose you drew this conclusion: no one will ever be hurt by hurricanes again. This might seem like a valid conclusion at first. The passage says that meteorologists' work allows people to prepare for hurricanes. However, you should think about what you know based on your own experience. You may have seen hurricanes on the news. They still hurt people. The conclusion is invalid. A better conclusion would be this: meteorologists' work means fewer people will be hurt by hurricanes than in the past.

Read the passage and draw a conclusion.

> Dogs can be trained to do many things. Some dogs are guides for blind people. Some dogs learn to find lost people. Farm dogs can learn how to herd cattle.

Did you conclude that dogs are smart animals? The facts support this conclusion. It is valid. You read facts about things dogs can learn to do. You know that animals have to be smart to be trained. You can put what you read and what you know together.

Did you conclude that dogs make good pets? It is true, but it is not supported by facts in the passage. That makes it an invalid conclusion.

Read each passage. Then circle the letter of the answer to each question.

> Who discovered coffee? One story says that it was a boy who herded goats. His goats ate some red berries from a tree. The goats became very active. The boy tried some. He felt more awake when he ate them. People soon learned how to dry and grind the berries to make coffee.

1. From the passage, you can conclude that when coffee was discovered,

   A people were afraid of its effects.

   B people were glad to find a new way to stay awake.

   C people had many ways to feel more awake.

   D people did not like to try new things.

2. What can you conclude about the discovery of new foods and drinks?

   F Most are discovered by scientists.

   G Often they are discovered by goat herders.

   H They were all discovered a very long time ago.

   J They may be discovered by accident.

Read the passage below. Then read each conclusion. If the conclusion is supported by the facts, write *valid*. If it is not, write a valid conclusion.

> People sweat, but dogs and cats pant. These are both ways to release heat. Birds pant, too. They also have other ways to release heat. Birds are very active. They build up a lot of heat. Birds can increase the blood flow to their feet to release heat from their body. They also rest during the warm parts of the day.

3. Conclusion: Animals keep cool in different ways.

_____

4. Conclusion: Birds rest in the warm parts of the day because they are so active.

_____

5. Conclusion: Dogs and cats are not as active as birds.

_____

Read each passage. Then write an answer to each question.

> A butterfly has no mouth. It can't chew, so it eats through a long, thin tube. The butterfly can suck up sweet nectar through the tube.

1. What can you conclude about the kind of food a butterfly eats?

_____

> An actor named Tom London holds a record. He was in more films than any other actor. He appeared in many western movies. He often played the sheriff. He played "good guys" and "bad guys." He started with small parts. Then he played lead roles. He appeared in many films in his lifetime.

2. What can you conclude about Tom London's skill as an actor?

_____

> Ambrose Burnside was an army general. He fought for the Union Army in the Civil War. He had no beard, but he grew long whiskers down the sides of his face. They covered parts of his cheeks. Soon other men began to grow whiskers like Burnside's. At first they called them "burnsides." Later the name changed to "sideburns."

3. What can you conclude about how Burnside's men felt about him?

_____

Read the passage. Then read the conclusion. If the conclusion is supported by facts, write _valid_. If it is not, write your own valid conclusion.

> Some people hate spiders, but spiders help us. They eat bugs day and night. There are millions and millions of insects on Earth. What if spiders did not eat bugs? The bugs would eat our crops.

4. Conclusion: If spiders disappeared, we would starve to death.

_____

Read the passage. Then circle the letter of the answer to each question.

Scientists start with small pieces of information and try to put these pieces together. They want to understand what the information means. Some scientists work with fossils. Fossils are the preserved remains of an organism that was once living. They may be old bones. They may be shapes of plants in stone. They may be other once-living things that have gotten hard. Fossils hold clues to the past. Scientists have been studying fossils for over 200 years. Fossils have told scientists much about life on Earth millions of years ago, but they don't give a complete picture. Fossils may hold important clues for scientists.

1. Readers can conclude that being a scientist is like being

   A a factory worker.

   B an ancient fossil.

   C a detective.

   D a painter.

2. Readers can conclude that fossils

   F are very valuable to scientists.

   G are easy to find.

   H are easy to understand.

   J were purposely left by ancient people.

3. Readers can conclude that

   A scientists will figure out the whole picture of life on Earth very soon.

   B scientists will keep working with fossils.

   C scientists' work with fossils has not been useful.

   D scientists won't learn anything new from fossils in the future.

4. Readers can conclude that fossils

   F are very old things made by people.

   G are only the remains of animals.

   H are only the remains of ancient plants.

   J are the remains of all kinds of ancient life.

5. Readers can conclude that

   A scientists will stop working with fossils once they really understand them.

   B scientists won't look for new fossils until they understand the first fossils they found.

   C it is difficult to interpret the information that fossils give.

   D fossils are not very complex.

Workplace Skill:
Draw Conclusions from a Chart

Businesses use charts to present information in a visual way. To understand a chart, first read the title. This will let you know what the chart is about. Then read across the first row and down the first column to learn what is being described.

Read the chart. Then circle the letter of the answer to each question below the box.

Health-care Career Profiles

Occupation	Training and Requirements	Salary Range
Home-care Aide	on-the-job training (high-school diploma or equivalency helpful)	$16,000–$29,400 per year
Licensed Practical Nurse	1 year vocational school OR 1 year community college after high school	$28,900–$55,100 per year
Emergency Medical Technician (EMT)	training program AND certification (high-school diploma or equivalency needed)	$19,400–$51,500 per year

1. Based on the chart above, which salary could you earn as a licensed practical nurse?

   A $16,700 per year

   B $22,400 per year

   C $35,800 per year

   D $56,500 per year

2. Based on the chart above, which salary could you earn as an emergency medical technician?

   F $14,800 per year

   G $19,300 per year

   H $23,400 per year

   J $55,000 per year

3. Based on the chart above, for which occupation do you need one year of community college or vocational school?

   A emergency medical technician

   B home-care aide

   C licensed practical nurse

   D none of the above

4. Based on the chart above, which position provides on-the-job training?

   F licensed practical nurse

   G home-care aide

   H emergency medical technician

   J none of the above

Write for Work

Your friend told you about her interview for a job as an emergency medical technician. She said that she went to the interview straight from her summer job as a camp counselor. She did not have time to change her clothes. She arrived 15 minutes late. During the interview, her cell phone rang, and she answered it. Your friend did not get the job. What conclusions can you draw about why your friend did not get the job? Create a chart of things to check off and things to avoid during an interview.

  # Reading Extension

Turn to "Flight to Freedom" on page 17 of *Reading Basics Introductory Reader*. After you have read and/or listened to the article, answer the questions below.

Circle the letter of the answer to each question.

1. From the article, you can conclude that Alina Fernandez
   A   wasn't a good mother.
   B   was strong and brave.
   C   left Cuba to find work.
   D   hated her father.

2. What can you conclude about people who live in Spain?
   F   They want to help Cuban people escape.
   G   They want to escape to live in another country.
   H   They have more freedom than people in the United States.
   J   They have more freedom than people in Cuba.

Write the answer to each question.

3. Reread paragraph 15. What can you conclude about how Alina Fernandez was feeling at the airport?

_____

_____

4. Reread paragraph 16. What can you conclude about Fidel Castro?

_____

_____

_____

Explore Words

LONG VOWELS WITH SILENT *e*

Many words with long vowel sounds have the same spelling pattern. They end in silent *e*. For example, read the words *cap* and *cape*. The vowel in *cap* has a short sound. The word *cape* ends in silent *e*. The *e* shows you that the first vowel has a long sound.

Read each sentence. Then circle the word in parentheses that has a long vowel sound to complete each sentence.

1. My grandfather needs a (can, cane) to walk.
2. His mother's skin is very (pale, pal).
3. Dalila has to pay a (fin, fine) for littering.
4. Will you give me a (ride, rid) to work?
5. I got a good (grad, grade) on the test.
6. What time does the (plane, plan) leave?

CONSONANT PAIRS

Some consonant pairs stand for one sound. The letters *sh* together stand for the sound you hear at the beginning of *shop* and at the end of *wish*. The letters *ph* together stand for the sound you hear at the beginning of *phone* and at the end of *graph*. The letters *wh* together stand for the sound you hear at the beginning of *what*.

Read each sentence. Then write the consonant pair *ph, sh,* or *wh* to finish each word.

1. Carmela took a _____oto of José and me.
2. I don't like the smell of fi_____.
3. Don't _____ake the bottle of soda.
4. The cart has four _____eels.
5. A _____ale is a very large mammal.
6. That dog should be on a lea_____.

COMPOUND WORDS

A compound word is one word made from two words. For example: *daytime* is a compound word. It is made from the words *day* and *time*.

Write on the lines the two words that make each compound word. The first item has been done for you.

1. whenever *when* *ever*
2. bedtime _____ _____
3. sunflower _____ _____
4. bathtub _____ _____
5. raincoat _____ _____
6. snowstorm _____ _____
7. playground _____ _____
8. wheelchair _____ _____

When you are reading, you may come across a word you do not know. Sometimes, you can figure out the meaning of the word from its context. To do that, look for words near the unknown word that give you clues to its meaning. You might find a synonym or an antonym that will help you.

Read each sentence. Then circle the word in each sentence that is a synonym for the underlined word.

1. The teacher thought a computer was <u>essential</u>, but most of the students did not think it was necessary.

2. She was helpful in a <u>crisis</u> or in any kind of emergency.

Read the sentences below. On the first line, write the word that is an antonym for the underlined word. On the second line, write the meaning of the underlined word.

3. Do you like <u>ornate</u> styles or simple ones?

   Antonym of *ornate:* _____

   Meaning of *ornate:* _____

4. Tyee does not like to be <u>idle</u>, so he is always active.

   Antonym of *idle:* _____

   Meaning of *idle:* _____

Knowing these high-frequency words will help you in many school subjects.

conclusions	decisions based on facts and knowledge
conclude	figure something out
valid	based on facts
invalid	not based on facts
supported	backed up

Complete the sentences below using one of the words above.

1. Your opinion is _____ because you didn't even see the movie.

2. After hearing the facts, the jury will probably _____ that she is innocent.

3. Do you have a _____ excuse for being late?

4. The article _____ my opinion of the city council's decision.

5. Before you draw _____, you have to pay attention to facts.

Lesson 1.4

Summarize and Paraphrase

A summary is a short restatement, or retelling, of spoken or written material. A summary should be much shorter than the original passage. A good way to understand a passage is to summarize it. To summarize a passage, tell only the most important ideas. Leave out most of the details. Read the passage and example summary below:

> An orchestra must have a leader. That person is called the conductor. He or she faces the orchestra. The conductor keeps time with a stick called a baton. The musicians pay close attention to the baton. It helps them all play well together. Without a leader, they would not play well together.

> *Summary*: Every orchestra has a conductor. The conductor keeps time. He or she helps the musicians play well together.

You can also paraphrase a passage instead of summarizing it. To paraphrase, use your own words to tell what a passage is about. A paraphrase may be about as long as the original, but it may use simpler words. When you paraphrase, be sure to include all the relevant, or important, ideas and details. Read the example below:

> *Paraphrase*: The leader of an orchestra is the conductor. The conductor stands in front of the orchestra. He or she waves a baton. The musicians watch the baton. This helps them play well together.

Read the passage. Then write a summary and a paraphrase in a notebook.

> Juan joined a new band. He plays drums. Every Saturday night, his band practices. His bandmates are funny. They are good musicians too! Juan likes playing with his band.

Was your summary short? Did it include only the important ideas? Your summary might be similar to the following: *Juan likes playing drums in his new band.*

Now look at your paraphrase. Is it about two lines long? Does it include all the important ideas and relevant details? A good paraphrase of the passage might be similar to the following: *Juan likes playing drums in a new band he joined. He likes his friends, who are good musicians and funny. They practice on Saturday nights.*

Learn to summarize and paraphrase. It will help to reinforce your understanding of what you read.

Read each passage. Then circle the letter of the answer to each question.

The ancient Greeks had many myths, or stories. One myth tells about the Gorgons, who were three monsters. The Gorgons were sisters. They had snakes on their heads instead of hair. They had flat noses and long teeth. Medusa was the most famous Gorgon. The Greeks thought that anyone who looked at the Gorgons would turn to stone.

1. Choose the best summary of the passage.

 A The Greeks told stories about three bad monsters called the Gorgon sisters.

 B The Gorgon sisters had snakes on their heads, flat noses, and long teeth.

 C The Gorgon sisters were monsters. They could turn people into stone.

 D The Greeks told stories about the Gorgon sisters. The sisters had snakes on their heads. They had flat noses.

2. Choose the best paraphrase of the passage.

 F The three Gorgons were in Greek stories.

 G The Greeks told stories about the three Gorgons. The Gorgons were scary sisters with snakes on their heads. Just the sight of them could turn people into stone.

 H The Gorgons were monsters with snakes on their heads and flat noses. They had long teeth. They were very ugly.

 J The Greeks made up stories. Some of the stories were about people, but some of the stories were about monsters.

Pigs are not stupid animals. Some pigs have learned to unlock gates. Then they are able to run away. Pigs can learn to do all kinds of tricks. They can learn to jump through hoops. Once a pig learns something, it never forgets.

3. Choose the best summary of the passage.

 A Pigs are stupid because they run away.

 B Pigs are not stupid. They can learn to do tricks and remember them forever.

 C Pigs often unlock their gates and run away. They learn tricks. They remember things forever. They can jump through hoops. They are not stupid animals.

 D Pigs are not stupid, but they do stupid things.

4. Choose the best paraphrase of the passage.

 F Pigs are smart animals that can do tricks. They can unlock gates even though they don't have fingers.

 G Pigs like to unlock gates so they can run away. They never forget what they learn.

 H Pigs are not stupid. They can jump through hoops. They can learn a lot of things.

 J Pigs are smart. They can learn tricks. They can learn to unlock gates and jump through hoops. Pigs never forget what they learn.

Read each passage. Then write a paraphrase of each one.

> Weeds cause trouble for garden plants. Some weeds take water from the soil. They don't leave any water for the plants. Some weeds wrap around plants and kill them.

1. _____

_____

> In the 1700s the king of Persia owned a famous diamond. He called it Kohinoor. The name means "mountain of light." People believe the Kohinoor is the oldest diamond in the world. It is now one of the jewels worn by the Queen of England.

2. _____

_____

> Snakes have narrow, forked tongues. A snake flicks its tongue out over and over. The snake uses its tongue to smell. The tongue "catches" odors and brings the odors back to the snake's mouth. Without a tongue, a snake would not be able to find its food.

3. _____

_____

Read the passage. Then write a summary.

> Once there was a man who was king for six hours. His name was Nizam, and he was a servant in India. One day Nizam saw the king fall into the sea. Nizam dove into the water and saved the king's life. The king was thankful. He said Nizam could be king for six hours. As king, Nizam ate a feast and gave money to the poor. He also had a special coin made.

4. _____

_____

_____

Read each passage. Then circle the letter of the answer to each question.

> The Komodo dragon is a real, live creature. It isn't really a dragon. It's the largest living lizard. This huge lizard just looks like a dragon.

1. Choose the best paraphrase of the passage.

   A The Komodo dragon looks real.

   B There is a lizard that looks like a dragon. It isn't really a dragon.

   C The largest living lizard is a dragon. It is located in Komodo.

   D The dragon of Komodo is really a kind of lizard that looks like a dragon.
         It is the largest living lizard.

> In the Stone Age, people got everything from nature. They used stone, dirt, and plants to make everything they needed. They hunted wild animals for food and fur. Today we still get things we need from nature. We make glass from sand. We make plastic from oil and other matter. We raise animals for fur and food.

2. Choose the best summary of the passage.

   F Stone Age people could not make many things.

   G Stone Age people used stone, dirt, plants, and animals for everything they needed.

   H Modern people are like the people of the Stone Age. We use things from
         the nature to make other objects. We raise animals for fur and food.

   J People today are very different from people of the Stone Age.

> People all over the world live in stilt houses. People build these houses over the sea. The houses sit on stilts. The stilts are like poles. The stilts are made of strong wood.

3. Choose the best summary of the passage.

   A Some people have houses in the sea. The houses have stilts. The stilts
         are made of strong wood.

   B Some people live in stilt houses over the sea.

   C Stilts are like wood poles. They are made of strong wood.

   D People cannot live in houses over the sea.

Workplace Skill:
Summarize and Paraphrase a Want Ad

You can find a job many ways. You can call friends. You can write letters. You can go to an agency. You can use an online job site, or you can use the newspaper. Most newspapers run want ads, either in the paper or on their websites.

Read the want ad and the hints underneath it. Then circle the letter of the answer to each question below the hints.

Want Ads

P/T Cook needed ASAP
Hours: 10–3 M, W, F
Exp. necessary, $9.25 per hr.
Med. benefits
Captain Fish Restaurant
145 Main Street
Vineland, IL 06038   EOE
hampton@reachme.com

Here are some hints to use when reading want ads.

1. Put aside time to read the want ads. If an ad interests you, mark it. Go back and read the ads you marked. Take notes on the important information for jobs you read online. Familiarize yourself with abbreviations used in ads. For example, ASAP means "as soon as possible."

2. Find out important details about the job. Ask yourself: Do I need to be trained? Will they teach me? Is the job full-time? Is the job part-time?

3. Look for the job duties. Ask yourself: Will I be able to learn the job? Will I like what I will be doing? Will I be able to do it?

4. Make sure you get the phone number or e-mail address. Know the name of the person to talk to, write to, or e-mail.

1. What is the best summary of the want ad?

A The restaurant is located in Vineland, IL.

B There is no experience needed for this position.

C The restaurant is looking for part-time help as soon as possible.

D The restaurant offers medical benefits and paid vacation.

2. How would you summarize number 1?

F Read the want ads carefully and take careful notes.

G Make notes only with a red pencil.

H Ask yourself questions as you take notes.

J Find out whether the job is full-time or part-time.

Write for Work

Reading want ads can help you find a job. Reread the four hints for reading ads on page 42. In a notebook, paraphrase the four hints in your own words. Then find want ads online or in the local newspaper. In a notebook, write a summary of five ads.

 **Reading Extension**

Turn to "The Heroes of Flight 93" on page 25 of *Reading Basics Introductory Reader*. After you have read and/or listened to the article, answer the questions below.

Circle the letter of the answer to each question.

1. Which sentence would you include in a summary of the article?

   A The terrorists wore red scarves on their heads.

   B The phone company official was named Lisa Jefferson.

   C A man screamed and dishes crashed.

   D On September 11, 2001, terrorists took over Flight 93.

2. Reread paragraph 6. Which sentence is the best paraphrase of the following sentence: "They vowed not to go down without a fight."

   F The passengers decided to fight back.

   G They hoped to win back control of the plane.

   H They thought their chances were very good.

   J They decided to give up.

Write the answer to each question.

3. Reread paragraph 12. Paraphrase the first three sentences of the paragraph.

   _____

   _____

   _____

4. Reread paragraph 18. Write a summary of the paragraph.

   _____

   _____

   _____

   _____

Explore Words

LONG VOWELS

The letters *a, e, i, o* and *u* are vowels. Every vowel has a short sound and a long sound. You can hear the short vowel sounds in these words: *sad, help, wish, top,* and *run.* You can hear the long vowel sounds in these words: *frame, Pete, mile, hope,* and *flute.*

Read each sentence. Then circle the word in parentheses that has a long vowel sound to complete each sentence.

1. Eduardo (rod, rode) in the back of the car.

2. A (glob, globe) shows the areas of the world.

3. We need a new (tub, tube) of toothpaste.

4. My son loves to go down the (slid, slide).

5. Do you know the ZIP (cod, code) for Detroit?

6. We walked through a (pin, pine) tree forest.

CONSONANT PAIRS

In each of the consonant pairs *wr, gn,* and *kn,* the first letter is silent. Each of these consonant pairs stands for only one sound—the sound of the second letter.

Read each sentence. Write *wr, gn,* or *kn* to complete a word in each sentence.

1. Tammy will _____ite a letter to Rashid.

2. Jin Ki fell and scraped his _____ee.

3. I got only one test question _____ong.

4. Sara _____it this scarf for me.

5. Did you _____ow the answer?

6. The _____at buzzed in the man's ear.

SPELLING: POSSESSIVES

Some words show possession. The words *Ray's book* show that the book belongs to Ray. Look at the *'s* in *Ray's.* It is used to write possessive words. Most words that end in *'s* show that something belongs to one person.

Read each phrase. Write a phrase using 's to show possession. The first item has been done for you.

1. the friend of Pang _____*Pang's friend*_____

2. the home where Yow lives _____

3. the story of the teacher _____

4. the coat of the child _____

5. the sister of Amari _____

Plural words name more than one thing. You can form the plural of most words by adding -s to them. For example, *computer/computers*. Add -es to form the plural of words that end in *s*, *ss*, *sh*, *x*, or *ch*. For example, *box/boxes*.

Read each word. Then write the plural form of each word.

1. actress _____

2. truck _____

3. tax _____

4. wish _____

5. kitchen _____

6. shampoo _____

7. index _____

8. skunk _____

9. pass _____

10. hoax _____

11. peach _____

12. brush _____

13. wrench _____

14. subway _____

15. bus _____

16. class _____

Knowing these high-frequency words will help you in many school subjects.

summarize   to retell the most important ideas in a passage

summary   a short retelling

paraphrase   to retell a passage in your own words

reinforce   to make stronger

relevant   important

Complete the sentences below using one of the words above.

1. Use easier words to _____ this short passage.

2. Please _____ the important ideas in two or three sentences.

3. Your opinion is _____ to this conversation.

4. Bataar bought flash cards to _____ his math skills.

5. This short _____ of the article makes me want to read the whole thing.

Lesson 1.5

Recognize Character Traits

INTRODUCE

A character is an individual in a literary work of fiction, drama, or narrative poetry. One character might be brave. Another character might be wise. Words like *brave* and *wise* are character traits. Character traits show what a person is like consistently. They can also show what a person likes or dislikes, or how he or she behaves.

Fiction authors give clues to a character's traits. They use several methods to show what a character is like. One method is narration. The narrator describes the character and shows what he or she is like. Another method is action. The author describes what a character does. A third method is dialogue. The author writes what the character says or what other people in the story say about the character. Writers of nonfiction also use these methods to write about real people. Read the example below:

> Alma works at the diner every day. She takes orders. She wipes down counters. She hardly ever sits down. "I like to keep busy," Alma tells a customer. Then she starts to make more coffee.

This passage shows that Alma is hardworking. You can determine she is hardworking by the things she does. She works a lot. She hardly ever sits down. You can also know that Alma is hardworking by the things she says. Alma says that she always likes to keep busy.

Read the passage below. Circle the letter of the answer to the question.

> As a young boy, Hans Christian Andersen spent most of his time pretending. He had few friends. He liked to play alone with his toy theater. When he was seven, his parents took him to see a play. From then on, he wanted to be an actor.

Which character trait best describes Hans Christian Anderson as a child?

A angry   **C** shy

B brave   **D** lively

Did you choose *shy*? The word *shy* describes what Hans Christian Anderson was like. You can figure this out from the things that he did. He liked to play alone. He had few friends.

When you read about characters or people, it helps to think about what they are like. Understanding a character will help you better understand and enjoy the story or article.

Read each passage. Then circle the letter of the answer to each question.

William Sidis was born in 1898. He was very smart. His father wanted to show how fast a child could learn, so he made William study math, French, and other subjects. At age nine, the boy finished high school. Harvard would not let him in until he was 11. At college, William was a whiz, but soon he broke down. He took a long rest away from school. When he went back, he was not happy. As an adult, William had no friends. He wanted to be left alone. He did not talk to his parents. He had many unusual interests. He died at the age of 46.

1. Which word best describes William's father?

  A kind

  B scared

  C pushy

  D friendly

2. As a child, William was

  F smart.

  G slow.

  H distracted.

  J lazy.

3. When he first went to Harvard, William was

  A a poor student.

  B lazy.

  C bored.

  D a good student.

4. Which word best describes William as an adult?

  F wise

  G unusual

  H artistic

  J bored

Long ago, a fictional king named Midas wanted to be wealthy. He loved gold more than he loved his own son. Then a spirit granted the king one wish. Midas wished that everything he touched would turn to gold. Soon Midas was rich beyond belief. Everything had become gold. There was nothing left to eat in the kingdom. The king's son cried with hunger. When Midas hugged the boy, he turned into gold! Midas asked the spirit to take back the wish and to give him back his son. The spirit agreed. Midas learned that the love of family is more important than riches.

5. Which word best describes King Midas at the beginning of the story?

  A jealous

  B greedy

  C unfair

  D creative

6. Which word best describes King Midas at the end of the story?

  F selfish

  G serious

  H wise

  J generous

Read each character description below the word box. Then, from the list in the word box,
choose two or more traits that describe each person. Write them on the line.

daring	wise	artistic	brave
creative	helpful	smart	bold

1. Clara Barton was a nurse. She risked her life to help soldiers during the Civil War.

   _____

2. George Washington was a general. He led a small, poor army against the British.

   _____

3. Grandma Moses was an artist. As an old woman, she taught herself to paint.

   _____

4. Thomas Edison was an inventor. He invented the light bulb and the phonograph.

   _____

5. Ernest Hemingway was a writer. He won many awards for his novels.

   _____

6. Sojourner Truth helped slaves escape to the North. She became a famous public speaker.

   _____

Read each sentence. Then circle the character trait that best describes each person.

7. Bobby bakes a cake for his friend's birthday.
   cruel   thoughtful

8. The firefighter carries a girl out of a fire.
   inventive   heroic

9. Kaia volunteers at the soup kitchen.
   caring   creative

10. Maria kicks over a trash can.
    angry   brave

11. Lester rocks the crying baby.
    nurturing   selfish

12. Rosie calls her mother every day.
    greedy   thoughtful

13. Amar is quiet and never takes chances.
    helpful   timid

14. Ryan never works hard.
    lazy   dishonest

Read each passage. Then circle the letter of the answer to each question.

> Muhammad Ali was a boxing champ and a great athlete. He had the speed and strength to play almost any sport. Ali chose to box. As a young man, Ali won an Olympic gold medal. He was the heavyweight champ three times. Muhammad Ali became known all over the world. Ali wrote funny poems, mostly about himself, but he had a serious side. He refused to go to war because he thought war was wrong. Ali lost his heavyweight title, but he earned the respect of many people.

1. Ali's poems show that he
   - **A** was a poor writer.
   - **B** had a good sense of humor.
   - **C** was very strong.
   - **D** was a great boxer.

2. Ali would not go to war. This shows that he
   - **F** was intelligent.
   - **G** had strong beliefs.
   - **H** was corrupt.
   - **J** was timid.

3. Ali was often
   - **A** likable.
   - **B** violent.
   - **C** unhappy.
   - **D** fearful.

4. Ali is best known for
   - **F** being a boxing champ.
   - **G** his poetry.
   - **H** losing his title.
   - **J** his beliefs.

> Ricardo does not like to decide anything. I want him to choose a movie to see. He cannot make up his mind. He usually just tells me to decide. Ricardo really doesn't care what movie we see. He is as happy seeing a romantic comedy as he is seeing a horror movie. He is the same about restaurants. Ricardo never cares whether we have burritos or burgers for dinner. Just don't ask him to make the decision.

5. Ricardo won't make a decision. This shows that he is
   - **A** not confident.
   - **B** decisive.
   - **C** critical.
   - **D** hateful.

6. Ricardo is happy with what others decide. He is
   - **F** critical.
   - **G** quick to anger.
   - **H** easygoing.
   - **J** stubborn.

7. Ricardo's friends must be
   - **A** generous.
   - **B** decisive.
   - **C** funny.
   - **D** serious.

8. Based on Ricardo's traits, he would usually prefer to
   - **F** do anything that someone else chooses.
   - **G** see a movie when he can choose it.
   - **H** go bowling every night.
   - **J** go to a club.

Workplace Skill:
Identify Character Traits for a Job Placement

Certain jobs require special character traits and skills. For example, a doctor should be caring and knowledgeable. A construction worker needs to be careful and skillful with tools.

Read the passage. Use context clues to help you figure out any unfamiliar words. Circle the letter of the answer to each question below the box.

Match Traits to a Want Ad

Carmela Rodriguez is married and has two children. She works at home but does not have a paying job. Now it's time to look for a job that pays a salary. Carmela started to list her strengths and abilities and thought of the kind of job she could do. Carmela isn't a college graduate, but she does have a GED credential. Carmela does not drive a car, but there is a bus one block from her home. A full-time job is probably too much for her right now. Carmela is reliable, caring, and takes good care of her children. She plays games with them. She changes diapers and keeps her kids' clothes clean. As a mom, she is responsible and serves healthy meals to her family. Carmela has even taken cooking classes at a health-food store.

Carmela used the local newspaper to look for a job. Here are the ads she found.

Landscaper	School-Bus Drivers	Child-Care Helper
Blue Hills Golf Course. Will train. Need own equipment. Apply in person M–F. 410 Hills Lane, Seattle, WA 93321	Full-time drivers. Clean driving record. Send letter. Attn. Saraj, Oak School District, 333 Yearly Rd., Seattle, WA 93443	Part-time day-care helpers. Work with infants and children to five years old. Child care exp. Call 406-555-1555 for an appt. Center downtown on bus route.

1. Based on information in the passage, for which job would Carmela be best suited?

   A school-bus driver

   B child-care helper

   C landscaper

   D none of the above

2. Camela is described as responsible. When someone is called responsible, it means that the person is

   F foolish.

   G angry.

   H disliked.

   J trustworthy.

Write for Work

A local company is looking for a child-care helper at the company day-care center. What character traits do you think that a child-care helper should have? Write three character traits in a notebook. Explain why you think these traits are important.

 Reading Extension

Turn to "Seeing for the First Time" on page 33 of *Reading Basics Introductory Reader*. After you have read and/or listened to the article, answer the questions below.

Circle the letter of the answer to each question.

1. Which character trait best describes Harun when he was a child?

   A hardworking

   B playful

   C sad

   D clever

2. Which character trait best describes Harun after his operation?

   F grateful

   G lazy

   H angry

   J mean

3. Which character trait best describes the children after their operations?

   A brave

   B joyous

   C selfish

   D smart

Write the answer to the question.

4. Describe the strangers who helped Harun. Include their character traits.

   _____

   _____

   _____

   _____

Explore Words

HARD AND SOFT c

The letter *c* has different sounds. In the words *cave* and *cat*, the letter *c* has a hard sound. A hard *c* has the same sound as the letter *k*. In the words *city* and *ice*, the letter *c* has a soft sound. A soft *c* has the same sound as the letter *s*.

Read each word. Write *hard* or *soft* for the sound of c in each word.

1. account _____

2. card _____

3. candle _____

4. palace _____

5. fence _____

6. place _____

7. candy _____

8. record _____

9. crayon _____

10. careful _____

11. race _____

12. officer _____

HARD AND SOFT g

The letter *g* has different sounds. In the words *go* and *give*, the letter *g* has a hard sound. In the words *cage* and *germ*, the letter *g* has a soft sound. A soft *g* has the same sound as the letter *j*.

Read each word. Write *hard* or *soft* for the sound of g in each word.

1. huge _____

2. large _____

3. gym _____

4. stranger _____

5. gift _____

6. long _____

7. game _____

8. goose _____

9. great _____

10. giant _____

11. goal _____

12. gentle _____

COMPOUND WORDS

A compound word is a word made by putting two smaller words together. *Football* is a compound word. It is made up of the words *foot* and *ball*.

Read each word. Put a ✓ next to the compound words.

1. _____ newspaper

2. _____ ashtray

3. _____ basketball

4. _____ regret

5. _____ wallet

6. _____ baseball

7. _____ sentence

8. _____ wheelchair

9. _____ bedtime

10. _____ common

11. _____ moonbeam

12. _____ subject

Some words have more than one meaning. For example, the word *set* can mean to put or lay something in a specific place. *Set* can also mean a group of things that belong together.

Read each sentence below. Put a ✓ next to the meaning of the underlined word.

1. Your <u>chest</u> may hurt when you have a cold.

   a. _____ front part of your upper body

   b. _____ a box to store things in

2. When you are sick, get lots of <u>rest</u>.

   a. _____ something left over

   b. _____ sleep

3. Oma stays healthy because she eats <u>right</u>.

   a. _____ correctly

   b. _____ opposite of left

4. Exercise helps her stay <u>fit</u>.

   a. _____ fix or put into place

   b. _____ strong

5. When her cold was gone, Lin felt <u>well</u>.

   a. _____ not sick

   b. _____ a place to get water

6. My brother is wearing an <u>orange</u> shirt.

   a. _____ a kind of fruit

   b. _____ a color

Knowing these high-frequency words will help you in many school subjects.

characters	the people or animals in a work of fiction
traits	the things about people that make them special
consistently	usually or always the same
clues	hints
determine	to figure out

Complete the sentences below using one of the words above.

1. I can't _____ which way to turn at the light.

2. Some of the _____ in the book are from another planet.

3. Can you describe some of her _____?

4. The police look for _____ to solve crimes.

5. She has _____ scored the most points per game.

Lesson 1.6

Use Forms

A form has blank spaces for you to fill in. Some forms are electronic and some are on paper. We use many different kinds of forms in our daily lives. We complete electronic forms to order things online. We fill out forms when we apply for jobs. Forms often use short phrases and abbreviations. It is important to understand these phrases and abbreviations. Then you can complete the form correctly.

Forms usually have blank lines to write on. They can also have lists with boxes next to them. The boxes are there for you to check. Some forms ask for your signature.

Follow these steps when you need to fill out any kind of form:

1. Read the whole form before you start to write.

2. Look for headings to see if there are different parts of the form.

3. Look for abbreviations. Make sure you know what they mean.

4. Use a dictionary to look up words you don't know.

Read the library card application form. Then answer the question. Do not fill in the form.

Number _____   Expires _____

_____
DO NOT WRITE ABOVE THIS LINE

I apply for the right to use the library. I will accept its rules. I will pay fines or damages charged to me. I will give notice of any change of address.

Print Full Name _____

Sign Full Name _____

Address _____

Phone # _____   Birth Date _____

E-mail (optional) _____

What should you write next to the word *Number*?
The answer is *nothing*—you should leave that space blank. Did you see the direction "DO NOT WRITE ABOVE THIS LINE"? You did if you read the whole form. Following the directions will help you when you fill out forms.

To request an interlibrary loan means to request materials from another library system. Read the interlibrary loan form. Then answer the questions. Do not fill in the form.

Patron Interlibrary Loan Request for Books

Loan Request Number _____   Date Submitted _____

_____

DO NOT WRITE ABOVE THIS LINE

Before submitting your request, please make sure that your library does not already own the book.

Author(s) (Last Name, First Name) _____

Book Title _____

Your Name _____

Library Card # _____   Phone # _____

E-mail (optional) _____

Today's Date _____   Date Needed By _____

Some materials are **NOT** available through an interlibrary loan. Please do not request textbooks, reference books, rare items, or newspapers.

---

1. What would you write next to *Loan Request Number*?

_____

2. You want to request a book by Arlene Taylor. How would you write her name on the author line?

_____

3. What can you request using this form?

   A books

   B newspapers

   C reference books

   D textbooks

4. Do you have to write your e-mail address on this form? Why or why not?

_____

_____

_____

Below is a form for signing up and paying for a computer course. Study the form and answer the questions below it. Do not fill in the form.

Complete the application form below. Enclose full payment with registration.

Name _____   DOB _____

Street Address _____

City _____   State _____   ZIP _____

Phone (_____) _____   E-mail _____

Fall Computer Courses:
☐ Beginning Word Part I (Mondays & Wednesdays, 1–4 P.M.)
☐ Beginning Excel Part I (Tuesdays & Thursdays, 6–9 P.M.)
☐ PowerPoint Basics (Mondays & Wednesdays, 6–9 P.M.)

COST: $75 due now for each course, plus a $20 book fee due the first day of class.
Fees are payable by check or charge. Please make checks payable to: **Glenview Adult Education**.
To charge, fill in credit card information below:

VISA/MasterCard Credit Card # _____   Exp. Date _____   Amount Paid _____

Signature _____
Please return this form and your payment to:
Glenview Adult Education
7971 N. Woodmere Dr.
Glenview, IL 60062

Circle the letter of the answer to the question.

1. The abbreviation DOB stands for

A down or back.

B date of birth.

C deed of bank.

D direct offer below.

2. The abbreviation "Exp." in "Exp. Date" stands for

F Experience

G Export

H Explanation

J Expiration

Write the answer to each question.

3. How should you use the boxes on the form? _____

4. What are the two ways you can pay for the computer course?

_____

5. What is the total cost for each computer class?

_____

This form is part of a lease. Read the form. Then answer the questions below it. Do not fill in the form.

Name _____ DOB _____

Current Address _____

City _____ State _____ ZIP _____

Current Monthly Rent $ _____ How long at this address?** _____

Current Landlord: _____

Current Landlord's Phone # _____

** If less than 2 years, please fill in the blanks on the next four lines.

Previous Address _____

City _____ State _____ ZIP _____

Previous Monthly Rent $ _____ How long at this address? _____

Previous Landlord _____ Phone # _____

List two personal or professional references for the landlord to contact.

Reference 1

Name _____

Address _____

Phone # _____

Relationship: _____

Reference 2

Name _____

Address _____

Phone # _____

Relationship: _____

1. What should you write next to DOB? _____

2. What should you write next to Current Address?

_____

3. What does Previous Address mean?

_____

4. Not everyone has to fill in the information about previous address. In what case would you fill it in?

_____

5. What is a ZIP?

_____

6. What is a landlord? _____

Workplace Skill:
Fill Out an Employee Record Form

Many businesses use forms. The forms help them keep track of information. Forms ask for facts. Before you fill out a form, first read it carefully. Forms take time to complete. If you don't have your facts, forms can take even more time. You may need to go back a second time to complete some forms.

Read the form. Then answer the questions below the box. Do not fill in the form.

Company Employee Record

Please print clearly.

NAME _____   _____   _____
       (Last)   (First)   (MI)

ADDRESS _____
          (Street Address)

_____   _____   _____
(City)   (State)   (ZIP Code)

COUNTY _____

HOME PHONE NUMBER _____
                       (Area Code)

WORK PHONE NUMBER _____
                       (Area Code)

DATE OF BIRTH _____ **PLACE OF BIRTH** _____

SOCIAL SECURITY NUMBER _____ - _____ - _____

ARE YOU A U.S. CITIZEN? Yes _____ **No** _____

If no, in what country were you born? _____

---

1. What is the purpose of this form?

   A   to keep a record of a company employee

   B   to apply for a driver's license in your state

   C   to make an appointment with a doctor

   D   to request a credit card at a major store

2. This form asks for what type of information?

   F   information on career goals

   G   information on computer skills

   H   information on education history

   J   basic personal information

3. In what case must you fill in the country where you were born?

_____

Write for Work

Your workplace is starting a baseball team. They have asked you to create a form to send to people in the company. They want to know who is interested in being on the team. They also want to know which night is best for most people to practice. Create a form in a notebook. Include space for the important details.

Workplace Extension

The Interview

Steve Brown was preparing for an interview. He had an appointment to meet someone about a job. Last week, Steve sent in his cover letter and résumé. The staff at his school's job center helped him write them. He included the names of his former managers. They would be able to tell a future employer about his work. He didn't ask the managers before he gave their names. He hoped they would give good reports about his work. For the interview, Steve chose a neat business suit and tie to wear. He tried to think of questions the interviewer might ask about his skills. He did not have time to practice his replies. He would just have to respond as best he could.

Circle the letter of the answer to the question.

1. The job center helped Steve Brown
    A select clothes to wear.
    B prepare his cover letter and résumé.
    C practice replies to questions he might be asked.
    D get reports from people he had worked for before.

Write the answer to each question.

2. Write two things you think Steve Brown did right in preparing for this interview.

_____

_____

3. Write two things you think Steve Brown should have done differently in preparing for this interview.

_____

_____

Explore Words

CONSONANT PAIRS ck, ng

Some consonant pairs stand for one sound. The letters *ck* together stand for the same sound as the letter *k*. The letters *ng* together stand for the sound you hear at the end of *ring*. The consonant pairs *ck* and *ng* can appear in the middle or at the end of a word.

Read each sentence. Write *ck* or *ng* to complete the word in each sentence. The first item has been done for you.

1. Mrs. Mendez said, "Good lu __*ck*__!"

2. Do you like the so_____ on the radio?

3. The girls like ha_____ing out at the mall.

4. Maria wrote a che_____ to the gas company.

5. Watch out for that tru_____!

6. I saw a brown du_____ in the pond.

7. She gave me the wro_____ number.

8. Put the money in your po_____et.

SYNONYMS AND ANTONYMS

Synonyms are words that mean the same or almost the same thing. Antonyms are words with the opposite or almost opposite meaning.

Read each pair of words below. Some are synonyms. Some are antonyms. On each line, write *A* for *antonym* or *S* for *synonym*.

1. hot   cold   _____

2. job   work   _____

3. talk   speak   _____

4. short   long   _____

5. buy   sell   _____

6. love   hate   _____

COMPOUND WORDS

Compound words are two words together that make a new word. For example, the compound word *cupcake* is made from the words *cup* and *cake*.

Read each pair of words below. Write the compound word that is formed by each pair.

1. birth   +   day   _____

2. back   +   pack   _____

3. hair   +   brush   _____

4. sun   +   shine   _____

5. blue   +   berry   _____

6. note   +   book   _____

7. grass   +   hopper   _____

8. bath   +   tub   _____

Some words with long vowel sounds end in silent *e*. For example, *time* and *broke* follow this pattern. Two vowels together can also stand for a long vowel sound. The vowel pairs *ai* and *ay* stand for the long *a* sound in *rain* and *play*. The vowel pairs *ea* and *ee* stand for the long *e* sound in *beach* and *greet*. The vowel pair *oa* stands for the long *o* sound in *soap* and *goat*.

Read each sentence. To complete each sentence, circle the word in parentheses that has a long vowel sound.

1. Pablo liked to (sail, jog).
2. Nicoli felt like having a (plum, peach).
3. The man picked up a (stone, rock).
4. There was a bad rip in his (coat, sock).
5. The old horse was (lame, fast).
6. The children (sat, played) all day.
7. Do you think it will be (sunny, rainy) today?
8. Please (give, feed) the baby her lunch.
9. I'm going to (Spain, Canada) on vacation.
10. He ate (toast, chips) for a snack.
11. Can you wear (pants, jeans) to work?
12. I can't (sleep, nap) during the day.
13. She carried a (tray, dish) full of drinks.
14. I thought the (price, cost) was too high.
15. The sun began to (dim, fade).
16. The car drove off the (road, path).
17. Minh (had, peeled) an orange for a snack.
18. Did you see the (bag, note) I left for you?

ACADEMIC VOCABULARY

Knowing these high-frequency words will help you in many school subjects.

form	a document with blank spaces for you to fill in
previous	earlier, going before
headings	titles, usually in dark print
complete	to fill out with writing
apply	to make a request

Complete the sentences below using one of the words above.

1. I have not taken any _____ computer classes.

2. I am calling to _____ for the job in the ad.

3. This _____ asks questions about your health history.

4. Do I have to _____ the section about past jobs?

5. The _____ on the page give important information.

Lesson 1.7

Use Correct Spelling

It is important to spell words correctly. Spelling is an important part of writing. You can improve your spelling. First, remember a few rules and a few spelling patterns.

Homophones

Homophones are words that sound the same. They have different spellings and different meanings. For example, read these sentences:

Your friends are <u>here</u>. Can you <u>hear</u> that music?

The words *here* and *hear* sound the same. However, they are not spelled the same, and they don't mean the same thing. Learning common homophones helps with spelling.

Adding Endings to Words with Silent *e* and Final *y*

Many words have a silent *e* at the end. When you add endings such as *-ing, -y, or -ed*, the *e* is commonly dropped. For example, read these sentences:

I can <u>make</u> a cake. I am <u>making</u> a cake for Rob.

Some words, like *carry*, end in a consonant and *y*. When an ending such as *-s, -est, -ed*, or *-ly* is added to a word like this, the *y* is typically changed to *i*. For example, read these sentences:

I can <u>carry</u> my bag. I <u>carried</u> my bag through the airport.

Words with Silent Letters

Some words have letters that are not pronounced. For example, in *comb*, the *b* is not pronounced. Remember the silent letter *b* in *comb*. Also remember other words with silent letters. Some examples of words with silent letters are *wrap, know, write,* and *lamb*.

Read the sentences below. First, circle the correct words in parentheses to complete the sentences. Next, underline the word that has a silent letter.

> Luis slammed his thumb in the door. Now he looks (pail, pale). Zada is (takeing, taking) him to the hospital.

Did you circle *pale*? *Pale* and *pail* sound the same, but they don't mean the same thing. Did you circle *taking*? Drop the silent *e*. Then add the ending *-ing*. Did you underline *thumb*? The *b* in *thumb* is not pronounced.

Read each sentence. Then write the underlined word with a new ending for the second sentence.

1. Did the baby <u>cry</u> during the night? *(-ed)*

The baby _____ until he went to sleep.

2. Do you like the <u>taste</u> of carrots? *(-y)*

Carrots make a _____ cake.

3. They decided to <u>marry</u> in June. *(-ed)*

They were _____ yesterday.

4. Don't <u>tire</u> yourself on the long walk. *(-ing)*

A hike through the woods can be _____.

5. Did you <u>save</u> me a piece of pizza? *(-ed)*

I really hope you _____ some for me.

Read each sentence below the word box. Write the word from the box that completes each sentence. Circle the silent letter in each word.

knife	wrist	wreck	gnaw

6. Be careful with the _____ when you cut open that box.

7. My dog loves to _____ on bones.

8. Are you wearing a watch on your _____?

9. Her old car is a _____.

Write the homophone that correctly completes each sentence.

10. I will help the child cut her _____. (meet, meat)

11. We will take a _____ when we go to New York. (plane, plain)

12. _____ is the book that I gave you? (Wear, Where)

13. This is my _____ Carlos. (son, sun)

Read each sentence. Write the word from the box that completes each sentence. Circle the silent letter in each word.

hour	sign	knee	climb	wrong

1. The store had a big _____ in the window.

2. The caller dialed a _____ number.

3. Would you like to _____ to the top of a mountain?

4. We waited for an _____ for the doctor.

5. He hurt his _____ when he jumped over the fence.

Read each sentence. Write a homophone from the box that correctly completes each sentence.

by	road	right	through	weak
buy	rode	write	threw	week

6. I went to the music store to _____ a CD.

7. The baby was too _____ to sit up.

8. Turn _____ at the next street.

9. The campers _____ horses every morning.

10. You will enjoy your walk _____ the forest.

Read each word below. Then write each word with the new ending.

11. try (add -ed) _____

17. copy (add -ed) _____

12. brave (add -est) _____

18. stale (add -er) _____

13. merry (add -ly) _____

19. cheery (add -ly) _____

14. give (add -ing) _____

20. freeze (add -ing) _____

15. smoke (add -y) _____

21. whine (add -y) _____

16. happy (add -er) _____

22. crazy (add -est) _____

Read each passage. Check the spelling of each numbered word. If the word is spelled correctly, write it on the line as is. If it is misspelled, spell it correctly.

Can you eat with (1) <u>you're</u> head upside down? Flamingos always eat that way. Flamingos look like pink swans. They have long, thin legs. They like (2) <u>living</u> near the (3) <u>see</u> or large lakes. The color of their feathers ranges from bright red to (4) <u>pail</u> pink. A flamingo has a large bill. The top (5) <u>half</u> of the bill is like a scoop. To eat, the flamingo turns its head over. It dips its bill into the water. With its (6) <u>comb</u>, it can be seen (7) <u>rakeing</u> (8) <u>threw</u> the mud for small animals.

1. _____ 5. _____

2. _____ 6. _____

3. _____ 7. _____

4. _____ 8. _____

Most insects are not good mothers. They have the habit of laying (9) <u>there</u> eggs and (10) <u>leaveing</u> them. They are not good at (11) <u>careing</u> for (12) <u>their</u> young. However, the earwig is different. An earwig acts like a (13) <u>loveing</u> mother. She stays with the eggs. She cleans them. When the (14) <u>babies</u> are hatched, she takes them to get food.

9. _____ 12. _____

10. _____ 13. _____

11. _____ 14. _____

(15) <u>Write</u> now, we are standing on a (16) <u>moveing</u> rock. You (17) <u>sea</u>, the Earth's crust is not solid. It is (18) <u>maid</u> up of huge plates of rock. (19) <u>There</u> always shifting because of forces within the Earth. Some scientists think that the (20) <u>great</u> heat inside the Earth causes the movement.

15. _____ 18. _____

16. _____ 19. _____

17. _____ 20. _____

Workplace Skill:
Use Correct Spelling in an E-mail

Coworkers often use e-mail, or electronic mail, in the workplace to communicate with each other. Always check your work e-mails carefully for spelling errors.

Read the e-mails below. Then answer the questions below the box.

From: Rosita Monroe, Human Resources Department
Sent: Friday, August 20
To: Ramla Stevens, Marketing Department
Subject: Draft of an E-mail on Company Blood Drive

Hi Ramla,

I need to send an e-mail about our upcoming Blood Drive. Can you do me a favor and read the draft below for any errors? Please get back to me with anything you think is incorrect. I did run the computer's spell-checker. Thanks!

Rosita

From: Human Resources
To: All Employees
Subject: Blood Drive

Our company will be holding a Blood Drive on Tuesday, August 30. The drive will take place in the lobbies of One and Too University Office Park from 9 A.M. to 2 P.M. All employees wishing to donate blood are required to sign up in advance. Please call the Human Resources Department to set up a date and time. You can schedule appointments online as well at humanresources@ caveltoolanddye.com

Our state has a serious blood shortage. Last year we supplyed 100 units to local hospitals. This year we hope to collect 200 units. Please help a worthy cause.

---

1. Which word from the e-mail has an ending that is not spelled correctly?

  A holding

  B located

  C wishing

  D supplyed

2. Why might the spell-checker not have noticed that *Too* University Office Park was incorrect?

  F The word *too* means exactly the same as *two*.

  G Both *too* and *two* are correctly spelled words.

  H The word *two* means the exact opposite of *too*.

  J The spell-checker is not working properly.

3. What are two ways that employees who wish to donate blood can sign up?

_____

_____

Write for Work

In a notebook, write an e-mail to your coworkers. The purpose of the e-mail is to inform employees about a meeting you have planned to discuss ways to cut costs in the workplace. Trade papers with a partner and check for spelling errors.

Workplace Extension

Call Ahead

There are forms for school. There are forms for getting help. There are forms to fill out for a job. There are forms at the hospital. You can't always know what will be asked. However, there are facts that you are almost always asked. For example: your name, your address, your phone number, and your date of birth.

Julie Graham was going to fill out an application for a bank position. She wasn't sure what would be required. She called ahead. She asked questions. The bank manager told her she needed to bring a form of ID. Julie brought her social security card with her.

Circle the letter of the answer to each question.

1. What fact that you might put on a form was not mentioned in the passage?

   A your name

   B your address

   C your signature

   D your phone number

2. What did Julie do that showed good planning?

   F She filled out a form.

   G She called ahead to get information.

   H She arrived at the bank with no ID.

   J She wasn't sure what was required.

Write the answer to each question.

3. What might have happened if Julie had not brought what was needed for the application?

   _____

   _____

4. What other forms of ID might a workplace accept?

   _____

   _____

Explore Words

LONG *i*, SPELLED *-y*

Many words end with the letter *y*. Final *y* can stand for the long *i* sound, as in *cry*.

Put a ✓ next to each word that ends with a long *i* sound.

1. plenty _____   **5.** any _____   **9.** key _____

2. tiny _____   **6.** try _____   **10.** fry _____

3. sky _____   **7.** healthy _____   **11.** silly _____

4. spry _____   **8.** hardly _____   **12.** pry _____

LONG *e*, SPELLED *-y*

Many words end with the letter *y*. Final *y* can stand for the long *e* sound, as in *party*.

Put a ✓ next to each word that ends with a long *e* sound.

1. why _____   **5.** lobby _____   **9.** navy _____

2. shiny _____   **6.** try _____   **10.** my _____

3. reply _____   **7.** fry _____   **11.** ugly _____

4. dusty _____   **8.** pretty _____   **12.** many _____

PREFIXES *un-*, *re-*

A prefix is a word part that can be added to the beginning of a word. When you add a prefix to a word, the word changes meaning. *Un-* and *re-* are prefixes.

un- means "not"   *re-* means "again"

un + able   We are **unable** to pay this bill. *Unable* means "not able."
re + do   James will **redo** his budget. *Redo* means "do again."

For each word below, form a new word by adding the prefix *un-* or *re-*. Write a sentence using each new word.

1. _____certain _____

2. _____known _____

3. _____fill _____

4. _____read _____

CONTEXT CLUES

When you are reading, you may find a word you do not know. Sometimes you can figure out the meaning of the word from its context. To do that, look for words near the unknown word that give you clues to its meaning. You might find a definition that will help you. You might find a synonym or an antonym for the unknown word.

Read each sentence and look for context clues. Then write the meaning of the underlined word on the line.

1. Kojo was <u>drowsy</u> on the train, but I was wide awake. _____

2. Loud music <u>irked</u> him, but barking dogs didn't bother him at all. _____

3. Many people helped to <u>construct</u>, or to build, the bridge. _____

4. Elvio <u>enrolled</u> in English classes. He also signed up for computer lessons. _____

5. He was <u>glum</u>, and his friends did not know why he was so sad. _____

6. The farmers <u>exported</u> some of their corn, sending it to other countries. _____

7. How much do you <u>estimate</u> it will cost? My guess is about 25 dollars. _____

8. Isn't the <u>foliage</u> beautiful? The leaves are so colorful this year! _____

ACADEMIC VOCABULARY

Knowing these high-frequency words will help you in many school subjects.

common   seen often

pattern   an arrangement of parts that happens repeatedly

typically   usually

examples   things shown as models

context   words that help explain meaning

Complete the sentences below using one of the words above.

1. You can use _____ to understand what new words mean.

2. Text messaging has become a _____ way to talk to friends.

3. We _____ go to a movie on Sunday afternoon.

4. Tulips and roses are _____ of flowers I like.

5. A silent *e* is often at the end of words with a long vowel sound. That is a spelling _____.

Unit 1 Review

Recognize and Recall Details

Details can be specific facts. Details can also describe a person, a place, or a thing. Note the details as you read.

Understand Stated Concepts

Often concepts and facts are stated directly. When you can identify directly stated concepts in the text, you will better understand what you read. Bold print, headings, and titles can also give clues to meaning.

Draw Conclusions

Some facts and ideas are stated directly in a passage. Sometimes ideas are not stated directly. You can figure them out. You can put together what is stated with things you already know. When you do this, you can draw conclusions.

Summarize and Paraphrase

When you summarize a passage, you retell its main ideas. When you paraphrase, you put a sentence or a paragraph into your own words. A summary is usually much shorter than a paraphrase.

Recognize Character Traits

An author may show character traits by telling what a character looks like, says, or does. The author may also tell what other people think or say about the character. Writers of nonfiction also use these methods to show character traits of real people.

Use Forms

A form is a document with blank spaces that needs to be completed. There are forms to apply for a job, join a group, or ask for information. Make sure you know what the headings and abbreviations mean.

Use Correct Spelling

It is important to spell words correctly. It helps people understand the meaning of your words. Here are a few key rules and spelling patterns:
- Homophones are words that sound the same but have different spellings and meanings.
- When you add endings such as -*ing*, -*y*, or -*ed*, to words that end in a silent *e*, you will usually drop the *e* before adding the ending.
- Some words have silent letters that are not pronounced. The *b* in *comb* is a silent letter.

Reading Basics · Introductory

Unit 1 Assessment

Read each passage. Then circle the letter of the answer to each question.

> Where do hurricanes get their names? The weather agency of the United Nations keeps lists of names. The lists include the names of men and women. The agency uses these lists to name storms. Names are given in alphabetical order. For example, the first storm of the year gets the name that starts with A.

1. According to this passage, who makes up hurricane names?

  A a TV weather reporter

  B the weather agency of the United Nations

  C the president of the United States

  D the people in the country where the storm occurs

2. Hurricanes are named

  F in alphabetical order by when they occur.

  G with the same letter as the month in which they occur.

  H after a person from the weather agency.

  J after famous people.

> Where did the umbrella come from? No one knows for sure, but we do know that the Greeks and Romans used them. *Umbrella* means "little area of shade" in Latin. The Greeks used umbrellas to block the hot sun. The Romans used umbrellas on rainy days. For many years, people stopped using umbrellas. Then hundreds of years later, people in Europe started using umbrellas to block the rain.

3. Greeks used umbrellas

  A as sunshades.

  B as weapons.

  C to keep people dry.

  D to carry packages.

4. Choose the best paraphrase of the last sentence in the paragraph.

  F People have used umbrellas for hundreds of years.

  G Umbrellas are only used in Europe.

  H It is not hot and sunny in Europe.

  J People in Europe began to use umbrellas to stay dry.

5. Who invented the umbrella?

  A people in Europe

  B no one knows

  C the Greeks

  D the Romans

6. You can conclude from the passage that some English words

  F were not used in Europe.

  G mean many different things.

  H are not understood in Europe.

  J come from Greek and Latin words.

Would you like to save water? Then do not take a bath. A quick shower will get you clean. Some people think showers waste water. They say that the water hits your body once. Then it runs down the drain. Bath water stays in the tub until you let it out. The average tub holds about 40 gallons of water. An eight-minute shower uses only about 20 gallons of water.

7. What conclusion can you draw from this paragraph?

   A   Baths get you cleaner than showers.

   B   Taking a shower is quicker than taking a bath.

   C   An eight-minute shower uses about half the water used in a bath.

   D   No one should waste water.

Contact lenses work like glasses. They help people see more clearly. Glasses are worn on the face, but contact lenses are placed right on the eye. They do not cover the face. In a survey, people were asked how contact lenses changed their lives. Some people thought they looked better in them than with glasses. Some said they did better in sports. Some felt more confident overall.

8. Choose the best summary of this passage.

   F   Some contact lens wearers have done well in sports.

   G   Contact lenses are almost the same as glasses.

   H   You see better with contacts because you wear them right on your eye.

   J   Some people find that contacts have made their lives better.

Juanita, Allie, and Salim were planning a party.
"I don't know where to begin," said Salim.
"I'm not good at planning things either," said Allie.
"I've got some ideas," said Juanita. "Salim, you take care of the invitations. Allie, you plan the food. I'll take care of the music."
"Sounds good," said Salim.
"I'll get started right away," said Allie.

9. What word describes a character trait of Juanita?

   A   lazy

   B   organized

   C   confused

   D   forgetful

Read the form. Then circle the letter of the answer for each question below the box.

Member ID # _____ *7-28* _____	$100 Fee Paid (yes) no
Approved by _____ *Andrew Jensen* _____	
Activation Date _____ *2/1* _____	

DO NOT WRITE ABOVE THIS LINE.

I apply for the right to join the HealthWatch Club. I will accept its rules. I will pay the $50 monthly fee on time. I will not allow others to use my membership card.

Print Full Name _____ *Lucy Martinez* _____

Sign Full Name _____ *Lucy Martinez* _____ Date _____ *1/27* _____

Address _____ *333 Poplar Ave. Memphis, TN 38105* _____ E-mail _____ *lucy@martinez.net* _____

Cell Phone Number _____ *576-721-3188* _____

Text Messages OK   yes   (no)

---

10. The purpose of this form is to apply for

F   a job.

G   a club membership.

H   a library card.

J   a credit card.

11. The amount of the monthly fee is

A $50.00.

B $15.00.

C $100.00.

D $25.00.

12. When does Lucy Martinez's membership begin?

F   January 2

G   January 27

H   February 1

J   July 28

13. Lucy Martinez can be reached by

A   mail and e-mail only.

B   cell phone and e-mail only.

C   cell phone and text message only.

D   mail, cell phone, and e-mail only.

Circle the letter of the word that is spelled correctly and best completes each sentence.

14. The department store is having its yearly summer _____

F   sail.

G   sale.

H   sal.

J   sael.

15. My grandparents were _____ right after World War II.

A   marryed

B   marryied

C   married

D   maried

16. I am _____ a trip to California.

F   takking

G   takeing

H   taking

J   taeking

17. The doctor put a cast on the boy's broken _____.

A   rist

B   wrist

C   wist

D   whrist

Read the e-mail. Then circle the letter of the answer to each question.

From: Reception Desk
To: All Employees
Subject: Sign-in Sheet

It is very important to sign in each morning. If you don't sign in,
• You could miss an important phone call from a customer.
• Your boss may not be able to find you.
• You might not get your paycheck.
• Your coworkers might worry about you!

18. Who needs to know you are at the office?

   F   your boss

   G   your customers

   H   your fellow employees

   J   all of the above

19. Where did the e-mail come from?

   A   the reception desk

   B   the boss's office

   C   the mail room

   D   the copy room

Read the announcement. Then circle the letter of the answer to each question.

Flu Shots

Flu shots will be available in this office next Monday, October 3. If you are interested, please sign up at the reception desk. You must choose an appointment time when you sign up.

Note: The company will pay the $15 cost of the flu shot.

Flu shots can keep you healthy, so don't forget to sign up today!

20. Flu shots will be available

   F   every Monday.

   G   on Monday, October 3.

   H   today.

   J   last Monday.

21. What is the best paraphrase of the last sentence of the announcement?

   A   Sign up for your flu shot so you can stay healthy.

   B   You can stay well if you forget to sign up for your flu shot.

   C   Flu shots are very important.

   D   Staying healthy is very important.

22. You can get a flu shot if you

   F   pay $15.

   G   come to the office on Monday.

   H   sign up for an appointment.

   J   ask your boss.

23. Based on the announcement, you can conclude that the company

   A   wants people to work even if they are sick.

   B   will go out of business if too many people get the flu.

   C   does not care about employee health.

   D   wants employees to get flu shots in order to stay healthy.

Read the bulletin board notice. Then circle the letter of the answer to each question below the box.

Jury Duty Notice

To: All Employees
From: Human Resources

Have you been called to jury duty? You may receive a letter in the mail from the government.
If you do, follow all the instructions. Here are a few common questions and answers:

Q: Do I have to respond to the letter I get in the mail?
A: Yes, that's the law.

Q: Who needs to know that I have jury duty?
A: First tell your boss. You should also tell Human Resources.

Q: Will this count as vacation time?
A: No. Jury duty is special. The company has to give you the time off.

24. People must respond to a jury duty letter

F sometimes.

G if they have vacation time left.

H in all cases.

J only if their employer agrees.

25. If you are called to jury duty, you need to tell

A your friends.

B your boss.

C the postal carrier.

D the neighbors.

Read the schedule. Then circle the letter of the answer to each question.

Weekend Schedule

Employee	Saturday	Sunday
Emiko	Fill Orders	Take Orders
Juma	Take Orders	Fill Orders
Tito	Check Orders	Check Orders
Fred	Shipping	Shipping

26. Who fills orders on Sunday?

F Juma

G Emiko

H Tito

J Fred

27. Who always checks the orders?

A Fred

B Emiko

C Juma

D Tito

Circle the letter of the answer to each question.

28. Which word has a short vowel sound?

   F tile

   G end

   H feel

   J cube

29. Which word has a long vowel sound?

   A lunch

   B sprint

   C dentist

   D grain

30. Which word has a soft *g* sound?

   F gate

   G globe

   H margin

   J tag

31. Which word has a hard *c* sound?

   A icy

   B cabin

   C piece

   D center

32. Which word is a compound word?

   F bathroom

   G under

   H bravery

   J prepare

33. Which word is a contraction?

   A she

   B hers

   C she's

   D shes

34. Which is the correct form of the possessive?

   F Lenas book

   G Lena of book

   H Lena book

   J Lena's book

35. Which is a synonym for *lovely*?

   A pretty

   B lively

   C scared

   D poor

36 Which is an antonym for *strong*?

   F healthy

   G weak

   H sturdy

   J tough

37. What is the meaning of *repay*?

   A pay after

   B pay back

   C pay less

   D pay before

38. Which word begins with a consonant blend?

   F shelf

   G seaside

   H promise

   J children

39. Which word has a silent letter?

   A regain

   B design

   C signal

   D willing

40. I feel so <u>lethargic</u> today. Being so sleepy usually means that I'm getting sick.

The word *lethargic* means

   F chilly

   G uninterested

   H excited

   J sleepy

Unit 2

In this unit you will learn how to

You will practice the following workplace skills

You will also learn new words and their meanings and put your reading skills to work in written activities. You will get additional reading practice in *Reading Basics Introductory Reader.*

Lesson 2.1

Find the Main Idea

The main idea of a passage is what the passage is about. Often the main idea is stated in the first sentence. The location of the main idea can vary, though. It might come at the end of a passage or somewhere in the middle. Read the example. The main idea is the first sentence, and all the other sentences support it.

> Michie had a bad day at work. She missed the bus, so she was late. She spilled coffee on her blouse. Her first table yelled at her for bringing the wrong kind of fries. Her second table didn't leave a tip. Her boss yelled at her for being too slow rolling silverware.

The main idea of this passage is, "Michie had a bad day at work." Every sentence that follows gives details about why Michie's day as a waitress was bad.

Sometimes the main idea is implied. That means that it is not stated directly. You need to figure it out from the details. Try to identify the main idea of a passage. Then check to see if all the details support the main idea. If not, try restating the main idea in a different way. Read the example passage:

> A group of lions is called a pride. A pride is made up of a few males, several females, and cubs. Some of the pride members hunt for food in one spot. Some hunt in another. A pride hunts in an area of 8 to 150 square miles. Strangers that enter the pride's grounds are chased out or killed.

The main idea is not stated directly in the passage, but you can figure it out from the details. The main idea could be stated, "Lions live and work together in a group." The details give the name for a group of lions, how many animals are in a pride, and how they hunt. The main idea connects all the details.

Underline the main idea in the following passage:

> Linen is a light, woven cloth made from the stems of the flax plant. The stalks of the plant are dried. Then they are soaked in water. They are dried again. Then the fibers are taken from the stems. The finest fibers are used for weaving. Linen is used for summer clothing and tablecloths.

You should have underlined the first sentence. All of the details that follow support that main idea.

Read each passage. One sentence in the passage best states the main idea. Write that sentence on the lines.

Crows are clever birds. They can get food away from a dog. A team of three crows dives toward a dog that has food. Then two crows fly about to confuse the dog. The third crow dashes in and takes the food.

1. _____

_____

Fiddler crabs are shellfish that live on beaches. Their name comes from the large claw of the male crab. He holds it as if it were a violin, or fiddle. Female fiddlers have two small claws, but the male has one small one and one large one.

2. _____

_____

In August 1926 New York City held a big parade for a 19-year-old American named Gertrude Ederle. Ederle was the first woman to swim across the English Channel. She beat the record by two hours. She swam across in 14 hours and 31 minutes. It was a 35-mile swim. The waves were rough, and the water was cold. Darkness fell while she was still swimming.

3. _____

_____

Angora rabbits look like large cotton balls with tiny faces. Their owners comb them often. Several times a year, the rabbits are sheared like sheep. Their fur is used to make angora yarn. The yarn is valued for its silkiness. Angora rabbits are a valuable source of fine yarn.

4. _____

_____

Read each passage. In your own words, state the main idea of each passage.

People don't talk with words alone. Our faces, clothes, and movements also say things about us. Animals also send messages in many ways. Not only do they make sounds, but their color, smell, and bodies speak clearly. Bees "talk" about food by the way they move. They do a dance that tells other bees where to find food. Whales "talk" with lovely songs. The songs travel well underwater.

1. _____

_____

Many animals have a tail. Some animals use their tails as an extra arm. Monkeys use their tails to keep them steady in trees. Cows swat flies with their tails. Fish use their tails to swim. Foxes have bushy tails. They put their tails on their paws and noses at night. This keeps them warm.

2. _____

_____

Although many birds eat seeds, birds eat other things too. Geese love grass. Woodpeckers find bugs in tree trunks. Other birds hunt for bugs among the leaves. Still others pull worms from the ground.

3. _____

_____

Both meat and dairy products come from animals. People who are vegans do not eat meat or dairy products. Bees make honey. Vegans do not eat honey either. They know that fruits, vegetables, and seeds contain enough protein and vitamins for a healthy diet.

4. _____

_____

Read each passage. Then circle the letter of the answer to each question.

Birds often bathe in water, but sometimes they take a dust bath. A dust bath can really help a bird. Birds have oil in their feathers. The oil helps keep water off them, but too much oil isn't good. It makes it harder for a bird to fly. Birds roll around in the dust. The dust sticks to the oil. Then the birds brush off the dust.

1. What is the main idea of this passage?

   A Birds take baths in water.

   B There are many different kinds of birds.

   C Oil is bad for birds.

   D Dust baths are helpful to birds.

Today's doughnuts are round cakes with holes in the center. They are fried in cooking oil. The cakes were first made in Holland in the 1600s. They were called "nuts" because of their shape. Settlers from Holland brought the cakes to America. Later an American invented the doughnut hole. He cut a hole in the cakes so they would cook more evenly.

2. This passage is mainly about

   F the history of doughnuts.

   G Holland's greatest exports.

   H inventions from Europe.

   J how fried foods are made.

Underground trains are called subways. They travel through tunnels called tubes. Subways are one way to escape traffic in many of the world's big cities. The longest subway is in Shanghai. The second longest subway is in London. It is 220 feet deep, and the tube runs for 252 miles. The world's busiest subway is in Tokyo. More than 6 million people ride on Tokyo's subway trains each day.

3. This passage is mainly about

   A London's geography.

   B the structure of train tunnels.

   C some subways around the world.

   D city traffic.

Workplace Skill:
Find the Main Idea in a Mission Statement

A mission statement is a brief description of an organization's fundamental purpose and goals. It is meant both for those in the organization and for the public. Like other writing, business writing usually has a main idea. Sometimes there is one sentence that tells the most important idea. Other times, the main idea is not stated directly. You have to think about what all the details have in common to find the main idea.

Read the mission statement. Then circle the letter of the answer to each question below the box.

Mission Statement
Fresh and Fast Restaurant

Our restaurant, Fresh and Fast, will serve healthy fast food. We will use only fresh ingredients. We will cook food when it is ordered. No food will ever be made ahead or reheated.

Our team will give fast and friendly service. All team members will know how to take orders. They will know how to make all the meals on the menu. Fresh and Fast will have a full team working at all times. There will be no unreasonable waits or lines. All team members will keep Fresh and Fast clean.

Fresh and Fast will help customers make good choices. The ingredients for all meals are listed. All of our sides are healthy, such as salads and fruit. Some restaurants charge more for healthy sides. Ours are all one low price. Kids' meals come with carrots or fruit. Team members are happy to take special orders.

Fresh and Fast will make every meal a happy and healthy one.

---

1. What is the main idea of the whole mission statement?

   A There will be no unreasonable waits or lines.

   B Fresh and Fast will serve healthy and affordable fast food.

   C Team members can take special orders.

   D Fresh and Fast will use only fresh ingredients.

2. What is the main idea of paragraph 3?

   F Team members are happy to take special orders.

   G The ingredients for all meals are listed.

   H Kids' meals come with carrots or fruit.

   J Fresh and Fast will help customers make good choices.

Write the answer to the question.

3. What is the main idea of paragraph 2?

_____

Write for Work

Imagine that you are starting a small business. You have a goal in mind. You need to write a mission statement. In a notebook, write a topic sentence that explains your goal. Then write two or three details about your goal. Your mission statement will help people know what your business is about.

  ## Reading Extension

Turn to "Pigs to the Rescue" on page 41 of *Reading Basics Introductory Reader.* After you have read and/or listened to the article, answer the questions below.

Circle the letter of the answer to each question.

1. What is the main idea of paragraph 5?

   A Pigs hate fire.

   B Carder didn't recognize the signs of fire.

   C No one was hurt in the fire because of Iggy.

   D Carder thinks Iggy is a great pig.

2. What is the main idea of paragraph 12?

   F No one wanted to help LuLu.

   G LuLu used a trick to get help for her owner.

   H LuLu lay on her back to do her "dead piggy trick."

   J A man followed LuLu to her house.

Write the answer to each question.

3. In your own words, write the main idea of paragraph 3.

   _____

   _____

4. In paragraph 6, is the sentence "Honeymoon smelled the smoke" a main idea or a detail? If it is a detail, give the main idea of the paragraph.

   _____

   _____

5. Why is LuLu a hero?

   _____

   _____

Explore Words

HARD AND SOFT *c* AND *g*

The letter *c* can sound like *k* in the word *cash* or *s* in the word *nice*. The letter *g* has two different sounds. It can sound like *g* in the word *go* or *j* in the word *large*.

Look at each underlined letter. Write *k, s, g,* or *j* for the sound that the letter makes.

1. <u>c</u>ard _____

2. <u>g</u>eneral _____

3. re<u>c</u>ent _____

4. <u>g</u>arden _____

5. for<u>g</u>ot _____

6. re<u>c</u>eipt _____

7. <u>g</u>iant _____

8. <u>c</u>lamp _____

SYNONYMS

Synonyms are words that have the same or about the same meaning.

Circle the letter of the synonym for the underlined word.

1. <u>messy</u> basement

 A concrete

 B cluttered

 C finished

 D cold

2. win a <u>prize</u>

 F contest

 G argument

 H award

 J game

3. <u>confusing</u> question

 A easy

 B obvious

 C difficult

 D unclear

4. city <u>limit</u>

 F boundary

 G center

 H population

 J road

SUFFIXES *-er, -est*

You add the suffixes *-er* and *-est* to words to change their meaning. The ending *-er* means *more*, and the ending *-est* means *most*.

Add *-er* and *-est* to the words to complete each sentence.

1. Mimba is tall _____ than her husband.

2. She is the tall _____ person in her family.

3. Each day Carlos runs a little fast _____.

4. If he wants to win, he will need the fast _____ time.

5. February is the short _____ month of all.

6. February is often cold _____ than January.

Add -es to form the plural of words that end in s, ss, sh, x, or ch. Add -s to form the plural of most other words.

Write the plural of each word on the line.

1. candle _____
2. batch _____
3. book _____
4. card _____
5. mess _____
6. box _____
7. pencil _____
8. class _____
9. duck _____
10. rash _____

11. wish _____
12. tax _____
13. patch _____
14. bat _____
15. sandwich _____
16. ring _____
17. soda _____
18. table _____
19. kitten _____
20. tune _____

ACADEMIC VOCABULARY

Knowing these high-frequency words will help you in many school subjects.

identify to recognize

imply to suggest

restate to say something again in a different way

paragraph a distinct section of a piece of writing

vary to be of different kinds

Complete the sentences below using one of the words above.

1. The main idea of a _____ is supported by the details.

2. She could _____ her car by its license plate.

3. You should _____ your diet to get different kinds of vitamins.

4. The writer did not mean to _____ such negative things.

5. Deidre had to _____ the instructions so that everyone could understand.

Lesson 2.2

Identify Cause and Effect

How many times each day do you ask *why?* When you ask *why*, you want to know the cause of something. For example, think about getting a sunburn. You might ask: *Why did I get a sunburn?* The answer might be: *I stayed out in the sun too long.* Staying out in the sun too long is the cause. The effect is that you got a sunburn. Every cause has at least one effect.

Suppose you got caught in the rain without an umbrella. Having no umbrella might cause more than one effect. One effect might be that your clothes get soaking wet. Another effect might be that your shoes get ruined. A third effect is that next time you won't forget your umbrella!

Using signal words is one technique that writers use to show cause and effect. Some common signal words are *so, therefore,* and *because.* When you read, look for words that signal cause and effect. Read this sentence:

> People thought four-leaf clovers were lucky because they were rare.

In this sentence, the word *because* signals a cause-and-effect relationship. The effect is that people thought four-leaf clovers were lucky. The cause is that four-leaf clovers were rare.

Now read these sentences:

> Manuel didn't call to tell Ariel that he would be late. Therefore, Ariel got mad and left for the show without him.

In these sentences, the word *therefore* signals a cause-and-effect relationship. In this case, there are two effects. One is that is that Ariel got mad at Manuel. The other effect is that Ariel left without him. The cause is that Manuel did not call.

Circle the signal words in the following passage:

> The screech owl is well named because the adult owl's sound is a screech. However, young owls make a different sound. They hiss so their parents will feed them. They hiss until they are full. When they stop hissing, their parents stop feeding them.

Did you circle *because* and *so?* Signal words like these will help you identify cause and effect as you read. Notice the last sentence. There are no signal words, but the sentence does show a cause and effect.

Read each sentence. Then write the cause and effect for each sentence.

1. Hunters hide behind tall grass so that birds can't see them.

Cause: _____

Effect: _____

2. Fish swim in large groups. Therefore, they can protect each other.

Cause: _____

Effect: _____

3. In the 1500s tulips were worth a lot of money because they were rare.

Cause: _____

Effect: _____

4. The water in the lake froze over. Therefore, people could walk across the lake.

Cause: _____

Effect: _____

5. The father picked up the crying baby.

Cause: _____

Effect: _____

6. Most people stop eating when their stomachs feel full.

Cause: _____

Effect: _____

7. It started to rain, so the woman opened her umbrella.

Cause: _____

Effect: _____

Read each passage. Then complete each chart.

The red-cockaded woodpecker is in trouble. It nests in big pine forests in trees that are at least 40 years old. That is because the center of the trunk must be rotten so the bird's nest will be soft. Today, there are fewer than 10,000 groups of these birds left. That is because people cut down older pine forests to use the wood.

Cause	Effect
1.	The woodpecker nests in older trees.
People are cutting down the pine trees where the woodpecker lives.	2.
3.	People cut down pine forests.

Because they are tall, giraffes may serve as lookouts. Giraffes can see very well. A giraffe may see an enemy far away and warn the rest of the herd. The herd runs to escape the enemy. Herds of other animals see the giraffes run, so they run too.

Cause	Effect
4.	Giraffes serve as lookouts.
Herds of other animals see the giraffes run.	5.

Chances are you have never seen a California condor. That's because there are few of these birds left on Earth. People began to use more land for farms, roads, and cities. Therefore, that land was taken away from animals. Once condors became a protected species, their numbers started to increase.

Cause	Effect
People use more and more land.	6.
7.	The number of condors is increasing.

Read each passage. Then circle the letter of the answer to each question.

Wind is caused by the sun. Here's how it works. The sun does not heat the air evenly. The air is warmest close to the Earth. Farther away from the Earth, the air is cooler. Warm air rises. When it does, the cool air sinks and takes its place. Then that cool air is warmed, and it rises. This flow goes on and on, and this creates wind.

1. What is the effect of warm air and cool air changing places?

   A sunlight

   B warmth

   C wind

   D heated air

2. The sun causes wind by

   F making clouds.

   G heating up trees.

   H making cool air sink.

   J making unevenly heated air.

The first humans in North America got there by walking. This happened during the Great Ice Age about 25,000 years ago. The people walked along a land bridge across the Bering Sea from Asia. The sea level was lower then. The people were hunters. They made the trip because they were following wild herds. After a while, the Earth grew warmer. The Bering Sea melted, and the bridge was covered with water.

3. Why did people first walk from Asia to North America?

   A They were explorers.

   B They were running away from the Ice Age.

   C They were following animals that they hunted.

   D They were looking for somewhere warmer to live.

4. Why can't people walk from Asia to North America today?

   F People are no longer hunters.

   G The water level in the Bering Sea is higher.

   H They do not need to.

   J There are no more wild herds.

Workplace Skill: Find Cause and Effect in a Safety Policy

A safety policy is a company's written record regarding the health and safety of its employees. Because health and safety at work are so important, there are rules that require workers to avoid putting themselves or others in danger. Workplace documents such as safety policies include causes and effects. They tell what to do or what will happen in certain situations. These are some clue words that signal causes: *because, since, due to*. These are some clue words that signal effects: *then, so, as a result*.

Read the safety policy. Then circle the letter of the answer to each question below the box.

Safety Policy

Safety is important at Johnson's Roofing. Please take the following precautions:

Avoid Slippery Roofs: When the roof is slippery from rain, snow, frost, or dew, the best precaution is to wait until the roof surface is dry.

Ladder Placement: Make sure your ladder is set up at the correct angle. A wobbly ladder is dangerous. Use ladder jacks to attach boards to the ladder. This will help you walk or stand safely.

The Roof: Constantly inspect the roof and remove any possible tripping hazards. Tools, electric cords, and other loose items can all pose hazards and should be removed from the roof. Make sure you secure the edges of the roof so that tools don't slide off. A falling tool can hurt people on the ground.

Clothing: Wear proper shoes and gloves. Rubber-soled boots typically provide better traction than leather-soled boots. It is easy to cut yourself on a piece of metal. Have a first-aid kit on the job site.

Heat Stroke: It is much hotter on the roof than it is on the ground. Drink plenty of water and wear light-colored clothes to prevent heat stroke.

Remember to use common sense on the job.

---

1. What is the effect of having a first-aid kit?

   A It helps you if you forget to wear gloves and shoes.

   B It is easy to cut yourself.

   C You are ready if there is an injury.

   D It keeps you from getting cut on metal.

2. Why should you secure the edges of the roof?

   F so that tools don't slide off

   G so that the ladder is steady

   H so that tools will fall safely to the ground

   J so that you don't have to use ladder jacks or hooks

3. What is another example of "common sense on the job"?

_____

Write for Work

The owner of Johnson's Roofing thinks that safety procedures are important and necessary. Suppose you work for Johnson's roofing. In a notebook, write three reasons why you should follow the policies. Then write three possible effects of not following them.

 Reading Extension

Turn to "In the Line of Fire" on page 49 of *Reading Basics Introductory Reader*. After you have read and/or listened to the article, answer the questions below.

Circle the letter of the answer to each question.

1. What is one reason Rascon joined the army?

    A   He was born in Mexico.

    B   He had no money for college.

    C   He broke his wrist jumping off the roof.

    D   He was only 17 years old.

2. Why did Rascon stop treating the soldiers?

    F   He was afraid.

    G   He was bleeding.

    H   The helicopter arrived.

    J   The other soldiers forced him to stop.

Write the answer to each question.

3. What was one effect that Rascon's actions had on his unit?

    _____

    _____

    _____

4. What was one thing that caused Rascon to receive the Medal of Honor?

    _____

    _____

5. What effects did Rascon's actions have on Neil Haffy's life?

    _____

    _____

    _____

Explore Words

CONSONANT PAIRS *sh, th, ph, ck*

Some consonants come together and stand for one sound. The two letters together are called a consonant pair. The letters *sh* together stand for the sound at the end of *smash*. The letters *th* together stand for one sound at the beginning of *think* and another in the middle of *father*. The letters *ph* together stand for the sound at the end of *graph*. The letters *ck* never appear together at the beginning of a syllable or a word. This consonant pair stands for the sound at the end of *cluck* and in the middle of *chicken*.

Write *ph, sh, th,* or *ck* to finish each word. Make sure the word fits the meaning of the sentence.

1. Drink water when you get _____irsty.

2. I don't like the taste of mu_____rooms.

3. Let's take a walk toge_____er later.

4. I will plant a rosebu_____ by the steps.

5. A go_____er dug up the garden.

6. Mr. Gonzales is a tru_____ driver.

SYLLABLES

A syllable is a word part that has one vowel sound. Every word has one or more syllables. For example, the word *man* has one syllable. It is a closed syllable. It ends with a consonant. The word *panic* has two closed syllables. The first syllable is *pan*. The second syllable is *ic*. Closed syllables usually have short vowel sounds. Knowing how to pronounce different types of syllables will help you read unfamiliar words.

For items 1–8, match each syllable on the left with a syllable on the right to form a word. Write the letter of the syllable and the word you form on the line. For items 9–16, count the syllables of each word. Write the number of syllables on the line.

1. hel _____   **a.** im

2. den _____   **b.** on

3. lem _____   **c.** set

4. on _____   **d.** met

5. viv _____   **e.** pus

6. tid _____   **f.** ic

7. cam _____   **g.** id

8. com _____   **h.** bit

9. computer _____

10. fish _____

11. father _____

12. television _____

13. party _____

14. accident _____

15. field _____

16. underwater _____

You can add endings such as *-ed*, *-ing*, *-er*, and *-est* to many words. For example, look at these words: *wash / washed / washing*. The spelling of *wash* did not change when the endings were added. Now look at these words: *chop / chopped / chopping*. The word *chop* is a closed syllable that ends with a single consonant. When you add *-ed*, *-ing*, *-er*, or *-est* to a word that follows this pattern, you usually double the final consonant.

Add an ending to each word. Write the new word on the line.

1. ship + ing _____

2. fair + est _____

3. attend + ing _____

4. scrub + ed _____

5. sharp + est _____

6. glad + er _____

7. fish + ing _____

8. shock + ed _____

9. pet + ed _____

10. high + est _____

11. hold + ing _____

12. pour + ed _____

13. soft + er _____

14. trip + ed _____

15. eat + ing _____

16. loud + er _____

ACADEMIC VOCABULARY

Knowing these high-frequency words will help you in many school subjects.

cause   a person or thing that produces an effect

effect   a result or consequence

signal   an event or statement that causes something specified to happen

create   to bring something into existence

technique a way of doing something

Complete the sentences below using one of the words above.

1. The _____ of the crash might be faulty brakes.

2. The carpenter used a _____ that his father taught him.

3. I asked him to _____ a piece of art for me.

4. One _____ of getting better sleep is increased energy.

5. Holding up a hand is a _____ that we are ready for our bill.

Lesson 2.3

Use Consumer Materials

A consumer is someone who buys goods or services for his or her own use. We are all consumers. We buy, or consume, products and services that we need or want. For example, you might buy a DVD player or a clothes dryer. You might buy the services of a plumber, dentist, or painter.

It is important to read any papers that come with the products or services you buy. They may contain important information that you need for the use, care, or safety of your product. They may have information about the service you received.

A prescription drug label has a lot of information on it. It has addresses for the drugstore and the patient. It has the number of refills available. It has the name and strength of the drug. It also has instructions for taking the medicine. Sometimes it contains warnings with symbols whose meaning may not be obvious. To understand the symbols, you must read the text that accompanies them.

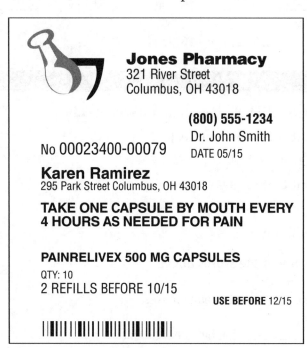

Jones Pharmacy
321 River Street
Columbus, OH 43018

(800) 555-1234
Dr. John Smith
DATE 05/15

No 00023400-00079

Karen Ramirez
295 Park Street Columbus, OH 43018

**TAKE ONE CAPSULE BY MOUTH EVERY
4 HOURS AS NEEDED FOR PAIN**

PAINRELIVEX 500 MG CAPSULES
QTY: 10
2 REFILLS BEFORE 10/15

USE BEFORE 12/15

Look at the label above and answer the questions.

How often should you take the drug? How many pills are in the bottle?

The directions are above the drug name. If you have pain, you can take one pill every four hours. If you do not have pain, do not take the drug. Look at the abbreviation *QTY*. This tells you how many pills are in the bottle. There are 10 pills in the bottle.

Whenever you take medicine, it is important to read the safety warnings and directions carefully. Over-the-counter medicine has directions for use and storage. It is important to read every detail on the label.

Read the label. Then answer the questions below it.

Drug Facts

Active ingredients (in each tablet)
Ibuprofen

Purpose
pain reliever/fever reducer

Uses temporarily relieves minor aches and pains due to:
- headache
- toothache
- arthritis
- muscular pain
- the common cold
- fever

Warnings

Allergy Alert: Ibuprofen may cause severe allergic reaction. Symptoms may include:
- hives
- facial swelling
- blisters

If an allergic reaction occurs, stop use and see a doctor.

Do not use:
- if you have ever had an allergic reaction to pain relievers
- right before heart surgery

Directions
- Do not take more than directed
- Do not take longer than 10 days without seeing a doctor

ADULTS AND CHILDREN 12 OR OLDER
- Take 1 tablet every 4 to 6 hours
- Do not take more than 6 tablets in 24 hours unless directed by a doctor

Children under 12
- Ask a doctor

OTHER INFORMATION
- Avoid excessive heat
- Use by expiration date on package

1. For how many days can you take this drug before you need to see a doctor?

_____

2. What should you do if you get hives while you are taking this drug?

_____

3. What should you do if you think your five-year-old child needs to take this product?

_____

4. You purchase this item on a very hot summer day. Should you leave the item in your car while you run other errands? Why or why not?

_____

Read the following advertisement for a new cell phone and service plan. Then answer the questions below.

1. How much money should you plan to spend if you want to buy the Carmel phone without signing up for a new contract?

   _____

2. Suppose you want to buy the phone and sign up for a year-long contract. How much will the phone cost?

   _____

3. Suppose you send at least 100 text messages per month and use at least 250 calling minutes. Would your texting and calling be covered in the $29.99 plan in the advertisement?

   _____

4. After you buy the phone and get a rebate form, what do you need to do to receive the rebate?

   _____

5. You have a phone contract with another company. You do not want to switch to USATalk. Should you buy this phone? Why or why not?

   _____

6. You already use USATalk for your phone plan. You have eight months left on your contract, and you do not want to sign up for any additional time. Do you think you will be able to get the discounted phone? Why or why not?

   _____

Read the following label for a beverage. Then answer the questions below it.

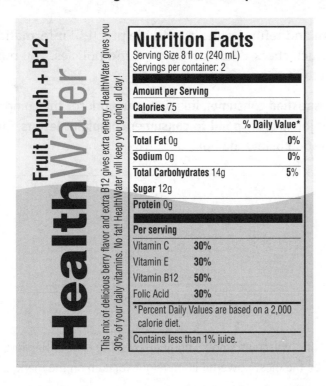

1. What does the abbreviation "fl oz" mean?

   A fluid ounces

   B full ounce

   C fifty ounces

   D flat ounce

2. What percent of your daily carbohydrates do you get from this bottle?

   F 5%

   G 10%

   H 14%

   J 30%

3. If you drink two bottles a day, how many calories have you added to your diet each day?

   A 0

   B 75

   C 150

   D 300

4. Read the sentences under the name HealthWater again. What nutritional fact from the label is missing in these sentences?

   F the name of the product

   G the amount of sugar in the drink

   H the amount of vitamins per serving

   J the amount of fat in the drink

5. If you drink the entire bottle of HealthWater, what percent of your daily folic acid will you receive?

   A 2%

   B 15%

   C 30%

   D 60%

Workplace Skill:
Respond to a Consumer Complaint Letter

Consumer materials such as return and refund policies provide practical information. If you are not satisfied with a product, check the return and refund policies. You may need to write a letter of complaint to the company.

Read the following letter from a dissatisfied consumer. Imagine you work for the company that makes the product. Part of your job is to respond to consumer complaint letters. Circle the letter of the answer to each question below the box.

February 29

Customer Services Manager
Peterson Vacuum Company
545 North Main Street
Hartford, CT 02903

Dear Customer Services Manager:

Last month I bought the Best-Clean upright vacuum (model number ZNC800) at your Hartford store. The vacuum was advertised to be the most powerful lightweight vacuum on the market.

I am disappointed with the product for a number of reasons. The main problem is that the vacuum bag is continually clogging. Dust accumulates even when the bag is half empty. The vacuum loses suction power. I must continually change a half-empty bag.

I took the vacuum back to the store. The person I spoke with said I could not get a full refund. However, your refund policy states that if there is a problem with the vacuum, it can be returned for a full refund. See page 67 of the policy.

I demand a full refund for the vacuum. I hope to hear from you shortly.

Sincerely,

Fred Hammond

---

1. What does the consumer want?

   A a full refund

   B a new vacuum cleaner

   C a gift card

   D an apology

2. Why is the consumer unhappy with the product?

   F it is the wrong color

   G it clogs

   H it is the wrong model

   J it is too heavy

3. What document does the customer mention?

   A the advertisement for the vacuum

   B the instructions for operation

   C the receipt

   D the refund policy

4. How do you know whether to give the refund?

   F See how much money the vacuum costs.

   G Call the customer.

   H Check the refund policy.

   J Try the vacuum yourself.

Write for Work

Imagine you are the Peterson Vacuum Company employee who has received the letter on the previous page. You have checked the refund policy and found that the consumer should get a refund. In a notebook, compose an answer to the consumer on behalf of the company.

 Reading Extension

Turn to "How Fast Is Too Fast?" on page 57 of *Reading Basics Introductory Reader*. After you have read and/or listened to the article, answer the questions below.

Circle the letter of the answer to each question.

1. According to paragraph 1, people with some conditions should not ride roller coasters. What is one of these conditions?

   A poor vision

   B weak heart

   C bruised leg

   D low weight

2. During which of the following might you feel a g-force of more than one?

   F sleeping

   G walking

   H reading

   J coughing

Write the answer to each question.

3. What is one way in which roller coasters can be harmful to people?

   _____

   _____

4. Why does Dr. Douglas Smith think that roller coasters are not to blame for riders' brain injuries?

   _____

   _____

   _____

Explore Words

Some words have long *i*, long *o*, or long *u* vowel sounds. Long *u* has two sounds. Say these words: *flute, mule*. You can hear a different long *u* sound in each word.

Say the first word in each row. Circle any other words in the row that have the same long vowel sound.

1. rude	fun	stump	blush	chute	rule
2. stove	plot	smoke	block	zone	rose
3. glide	gripe	drive	sink	risk	nice
4. fuse	cute	stun	fumes	skunk	music

A syllable is a word part that has one vowel sound. Every word has one or more syllables. The word *go* has one syllable. It is an open syllable. The word *refine* has two syllables. The first syllable is *re*. It is an open syllable. The second syllable is *fine*. *Fine* ends in silent *e*. It is a silent *e* syllable. Open syllables and silent *e* syllables usually have long vowel sounds.

Put the syllables together and write the word they form. Then underline any open syllables in the word once. Underline any silent *e* syllables twice. The first item is done for you.

1. re	bate	*rebate*	**4.** si	lo	_____
2. ta	co	_____	**5.** mi	grate	_____
3. ca	nine	_____	**6.** fe	male	_____

You can add endings such as *-ed*, *-ing*, *-er*, and *-est* to words. When you add an ending to a word that ends with silent *e*, the *e* is usually dropped: *hope / hoped / hoping*. When you add an ending to a word that ends in a consonant and *y*, the *y* is usually changed to *i: happy / happier / happiest*.

Add the ending to each word. Write the new word on the line.

1. amuse	+	ed	_____	**4.** thirsty	+	est	_____
2. prepare	+	ing	_____	**5.** funny	+	est	_____
3. lucky	+	er	_____	**6.** fine	+	er	_____

Reading Basics · Introductory

PREFIXES *pre-*, *mis-*

A prefix is a word part added to the beginning of a word. Adding a prefix to a word changes the meaning of the word. *Pre-* and *mis-* are prefixes. The prefix *pre-* means "before" or "earlier." The prefix *mis-* means "wrong" or "badly."

pre + bake   You have to **prebake** the pie shell and then fill it. *Prebake* means "bake earlier."

mis + behave   I told my son not to **misbehave** at school. *Misbehave* means "behave badly."

For each word below, form a new word by adding the prefix *pre-* or *mis-*. Then write the meaning of the new word.

1. spell _____

2. school _____

3. understand _____

4. paid _____

5. dawn _____

6. heard _____

7. apply _____

ACADEMIC VOCABULARY

Knowing these high-frequency words will help you in many school subjects.

consumer   someone who buys goods or services for his or her own use

text   printed wording

obvious   easily seen, recognized, or understood

instructions   directions or orders

accompany   to go with

Complete the sentences below using one of the words above.

1. You can't miss the sign. It's _____.

2. Kaan read all of the _____ reports before he bought his new car.

3. He read the _____ that went along with the album.

4. Aponi wanted to _____ Lomasi on her shopping trip.

5. Make sure you read the _____ before you use your new toaster oven.

Lesson 2.4

Identify Fact and Opinion

INTRODUCE

When you read, you need to be able to separate facts from opinions. Facts can be proved to be true. You can look them up or check them in some way. A fact is a statement that can be proved.

Fact   Carrots, beets, and potatoes are vegetables.

Fact   Apples, oranges, and cherries are fruits.

Opinions are statements of what someone believes or thinks. You may see words that can help you identify statements as opinions. These words include *should, better, best, worst, all,* and *like.* You can also look for describing words such as *beautiful, important, terrible,* and *surprising.* These often indicate an opinion. An opinion is a person's own idea about something.

Opinion   Potatoes are the tastiest vegetables in the world.

Opinion   Apples taste better than oranges.

If these clue words are not used, evaluate the sentence. Ask: Can this statement be proved? If not, it probably tells what someone thinks or believes.

Fact   James Naismith invented basketball in 1891.

Opinion   Basketball is more difficult to play than baseball.

Fact   Jorge thinks that baseball is harder to play than basketball.

Why is the last statement a fact? Jorge thinks something. It can be proved. You can ask him if that is what he thinks. Therefore, the statement is a fact.

Read each sentences. Write *F* on the line if the sentence states a fact. Write *O* if the sentence states an opinion.

1. Vincent van Gogh painted the still life "Sunflowers." _____

2. Vincent van Gogh was the best artist of the 19th century. _____

3. Vincent van Gogh was much more talented than Monet. _____

4. Vincent van Gogh died at the age of 37. _____

Did you write *F* for statements 1 and 4? These statements are facts. You can look up, or verify, the information in an encyclopedia or art history book. Statements 2 and 3 are opinions. Notice the words *best* and *much more talented.*

Read each sentence. Ask yourself if the sentence states something that can be proved. If it does, circle *fact.* If it doesn't, circle *opinion.*

1. Juan reads the morning newspaper on the train.

   fact   opinion

2. The guitar, the violin, and the harp are stringed instruments.

   fact   opinion

3. Earth's path around the sun is nearly 600 million miles long.

   fact   opinion

4. Some day people will live in space.

   fact   opinion

5. Satchel Paige was the greatest baseball pitcher of all time.

   fact   opinion

6. Light is a form of energy that travels in rays.

   fact   opinion

7. The National Air and Space Museum is the best museum in the country.

   fact   opinion

8. Wayne Gretzky is the highest scorer in the National Hockey League's history.

   fact   opinion

9. New York City is the headquarters for the United Nations.

   fact   opinion

10. Eleanor Roosevelt was the most influential first lady in the United States.

    fact   opinion

Read the paragraph. Then circle the letter of the answer to each question.

(1) Grebes are birds that can dive. (2) I think the grebe is the bird kingdom's swimming champ. (3) Grebes can swim at birth. (4) They build grass nests that float on water. (5) When grebe chicks get tired during a swim, they rest in air pockets under their mother's wings. (6) Grebes look like ducks with larger heads. (7) They are the world's most awkward birds. (8) Grebes often have difficulty taking off, but they can fly long distances.

11. Which sentence is an opinion?

    A   Sentence 1

    B   Sentence 2

    C   Sentence 3

    D   Sentence 4

12. Which sentence is an opinion?

    F   Sentence 5

    G   Sentence 6

    H   Sentence 7

    J   Sentence 8

Read each sentence. Write *F* on the line if the sentence states a fact. Write *O* if the sentence states an opinion.

_____ **1.** Many communities have shelters for abandoned animals.

_____ **2.** Some animals live in animal shelters.

_____ **3.** A veterinarian gives medical care to sick animals.

_____ **4.** People should be more responsible pet owners.

_____ **5.** Many pets are abandoned during the summer.

_____ **6.** It is not fun to travel with a big dog in the car.

_____ **7.** This animal shelter was founded 20 years ago.

_____ **8.** Anyone with free time should volunteer at an animal shelter.

_____ **9.** Anyone who adopts a cat or dog gets a month's supply of pet food.

_____ **10.** The vet, Dr. Wilson, is the kindest man in town.

Read each pair of sentences. Circle the sentence that is a fact.

11. Red and yellow are colors.

Red is a prettier color than yellow.

12. Dogs make better pets than cats.

Dogs and cats are mammals.

13. Jane Austen wrote the novel *Pride and Prejudice*.

She was the best English novelist of her time.

14. Sewage and chemicals from factories cause water pollution.

Factories that pollute water supplies should be fined.

15. Paleontologists are people who hunt for and study fossils.

Being a paleontologist would be a fun and exciting career.

16. You have to be brave to ride the roller coaster at the park.

Tivoli Gardens is one of the world's oldest amusement parks.

17. It's just foolish for anyone to travel without a map or a GPS.

A road map shows distance and direction.

18. Citizens of the United States have many rights.

U.S. citizens should appreciate the rights they have.

Circle the letter of the answer to each question.

1. Which sentence states an opinion?

   A A tiger can be seven feet long and weigh 500 pounds.

   B Tigers are the most beautiful animals in the jungle.

   C A tiger's stripes help it hide in its surroundings.

   D Tigers live in grasslands and forests.

2. Which sentence states a fact?

   F It's best to recycle paper, glass, and aluminum.

   G All communities should require recycling.

   H Americans throw away too much paper.

   J Some containers can be recycled.

3. Which sentence states a fact?

   A An ostrich is a funny-looking bird.

   B In some places, the ostrich is ridden in races, like a horse.

   C It takes a special kind of jockey to ride an ostrich.

   D It would be fun to ride a 300-pound bird.

4. Which sentence states an opinion?

   F Saturn's rings are made of chunks of ice.

   G Jupiter is the most fascinating planet.

   H Mercury is covered with craters.

   J Earth is 93 million miles from the sun.

5. Which sentence states a fact?

   A Thomas Edison invented the phonograph.

   B The zipper is the most useful of all inventions.

   C Everyone should have a computer.

   D Life would be boring without television.

6. Which sentence states an opinion?

   F U.S. coins are made of a mixture of metals.

   G Pennies should be taken out of circulation.

   H The Bureau of Engraving and Printing designs and prints all paper money.

   J Portraits of presidents appear on some American coins.

Write one fact and one opinion about yourself on the line.

7. _____

Workplace Skill:
Find Fact and Opinion in a Business Survey

Most workplace documents are based on facts. However, some may contain opinions or request someone's opinions. Look for clue words that show a statement may be an opinion: *think, believe, probably, perhaps, sometimes, best, worst, never.*

Read a company's customer survey. Then circle the letter of the answer to each question below the box.

Customer Survey

We would like to hear about your recent experience with our Customer Service Department. Your help in completing this customer survey will help us provide better service to our customers.

1. Name the product about which you had a complaint.

_____

2. When and how did you purchase this product?

_____

3. Do you believe you were treated with respect by the customer service representative?

_____

4. Do you feel the customer service representative was courteous and professional?

_____

5. How do you think we should improve our Customer Service Department?

_____

---

1. Which questions on the survey call for a response that is based on fact?

   A questions 1 and 3

   B questions 2 and 4

   C questions 1 and 2

   D questions 2 and 5

2. Which questions on the survey call for a response that is based on the customer's opinion?

   F questions 1 and 2

   G questions 2 and 3

   H questions 3 and 4

   J questions 3, 4, and 5

Write for Work

Imagine that you are an employee responding to a survey. The survey asks about a new child-care center for children of working parents. In a notebook, write three opinions about what this kind of center should be like. Then write three facts about working parents that help explain your opinions.

....

  Reading Extension

Turn to "The Mysteries of the Maya" on page 65 of *Reading Basics Introductory Reader*. After you have read and/or listened to the article, answer the questions below.

Circle the letter of the answer to each question.

1. Which of the following statements is an opinion?

   A The Maya lived in parts of Mexico and Central America.

   B The Maya were the best farmers around.

   C They knew how to drain low, wet land.

   D They built raised fields where they could plant crops.

2. Which of the following statements is a fact?

   F The Maya were great artists.

   G They made wonderful pots, rugs, and necklaces.

   H The Maya wrote books.

   J Perhaps their biggest talent lay in math and science.

Write the answer to each question.

3. What do you think was the Maya's greatest accomplishment?

   _____

   _____

4. Name two facts from the article that suggest the possible cause of the Maya's disappearance.

   _____

   _____

5. Reread paragraph 4. Find one fact and one opinion. Write the sentences on the lines.

   _____

   _____

   _____

Explore Words

LONG *e* AND *i* SPELLED *y*

When it appears at the end of a word, the letter *y* can stand for the long *e* sound, as in the word *party*. The letter *y* can also stand for the long *i* sound, as in the word *try*.

Read each word. Circle each word in which the *y* stands for the long *e* sound.

1. body
2. my
3. heavy

4. fly
5. any
6. why

7. try
8. bunny
9. funny

SYLLABLES

In closed syllables such as *pan*, the vowel usually stands for its short sound. In silent *e* syllables such as *cake*, the vowel usually stands for its long sound. Sometimes closed syllables and silent *e* syllables come together in one word, such as *pancake*.

Put the syllables together and write the word. Then underline any closed syllables in the word once. Underline any silent *e* syllables twice. The first item has been done for you.

1. tad   pole   *tadpole*

2. cave   man   _____

3. in   cline   _____

4. re   fuse   _____

5. fan   fare   _____

6. dis   grace   _____

7. pro   file   _____

8. dic   tate   _____

MULTIPLE-MEANING WORDS

Some words have more than one meaning. For example, the word *rose* is the name of a flower. It can also mean "went or got up." You can use context clues—other words in the sentence—to figure out the meaning that is intended.

Read each sentence below. Put a ✓ next to the word or phrase that has the same meaning as the underlined word.

1. Are you <u>free</u> to go to a movie on Friday?

   a. _____ without cost

   b. _____ available

2. I can <u>handle</u> any computer.

   a. _____ touch

   b. _____ work well with

3. I file and keep <u>records</u> at work.

   a. _____ disks to play music

   b. _____ written information

4. The doctor examined the <u>patient</u>.

   a. _____ sick person

   b. _____ able to wait calmly

SUFFIXES -less, -ful

A *suffix* is a word part added to the end of a word. Adding a suffix to a word changes the meaning of the word. The suffix *-less* means *without*, and the suffix *-ful* means *full of*. For example, *hopeless* means "without hope," and *hopeful* means "full of hope."

Choose a word from the box to complete each sentence. Then write the word on the line.

helpful	painless	forgetful	flavorless	skinless	thankful	endless

1. Rick had to write lists because he was so _____.

2. The doctor told the patient that removing her stitches would be _____.

3. Jennifer forgot to add the spices, so her stew was _____.

4. Kadar wanted to be _____, so he finished all the filing.

5. Tisa thought it was healthier to order _____ chicken.

6. When you can't sleep, the night feels _____.

7. We are _____ that we have such caring neighbors.

ACADEMIC VOCABULARY

Knowing these high-frequency words will help you in many school subjects.

fact   something that is known to exist, to have happened, or to be true

opinion   what someone thinks or believes about something

indicate to point out

evaluate to assess

verify   to make sure something is true

Complete the sentences below using one of the words above.

1. In my _____, winter is the nicest season of the year.

2. The _____ is that the dog has rabies.

3. Can you _____ that statement?

4. The signs _____ that Sofia will grow up to be a tall woman.

5. Winona needed to _____ the other employees based on their performance.

Lesson 2.5

Predict Outcomes

When you read, you can use clues in the story to help you figure out what might happen next. This is called predicting an outcome. Use clues in the text and what you know from your own life to make logical guesses about what will happen next. Here are some key points to remember:

- Make predictions before you read and while you read. Think ahead about how things might turn out.

- Use your prior knowledge and experience to help you make predictions. Ask yourself: Have I read or experienced anything like this before?

- Adjust your predictions as you read. Predictions should make sense with what you have read to that point, but they may not always turn out to be correct.

Read this passage:

Gracia pulled her car into the parking spot. She didn't hear the sound of glass crunching under the tires. When she came out of the store and started to drive away, she had a feeling that something was wrong with her car.

What do you predict was wrong? You read that Gracia drove her car over broken glass. You probably know that broken glass can cause a flat tire. You might predict that Gracia came out of the store and found that she had a flat tire. As you keep reading, you will find out whether you are right. Read the following passage:

Letitia adopted a new puppy on Friday. She named him Spud. The animal shelter told her that Spud likes to chew on shoes. All weekend she kept Spud away from her shoes in the hall. On Monday morning, she left Spud alone in the house.

What do you predict will happen? You may know that puppies can get into mischief when left alone. You might predict that Letitia will come home and find her shoes chewed up. As you keep reading, you will find out whether your predictions are right.

Use clues from the passage and what you already know to predict who will win the race.

On March 31, Li and Hyo both signed up for a mile race. They could both run a mile in about the same time. In April, Li trained two hours every day. Hyo did not train in April. On May 1, Li and Hyo lined up at the starting blocks.

Did you predict that Li will have a better time? It is likely because Li trained for the race and Hyo did not.

Use clues from each passage and what you already know to make predictions. Circle the letter of the sentence that best predicts what will happen next.

1. Paolo worked hard to improve his math grade. He turned in all of his homework on time, studied for every test, and even did some extra work. His teacher, Ms. Cook, said, "Paolo, I'm so proud of you. I couldn't have done better myself!"

   A   Ms. Cook will mark Paolo absent.

   B   Paolo will get a poor grade in math.

   C   Paolo will get an A in math.

   D   Paolo will forget to do his homework.

2. "Jafar," said Abeo, "do you really think we will be able to ride 25 miles? It seems like a long distance on a bike." "Quit worrying," said Jafar "Have I ever signed up for a bike ride we couldn't finish? Let's get going."

   F   Abeo and Jafar will start riding their bikes.

   G   Abeo will go home.

   H   Jafar will go home.

   J   Abeo will start to ride without Jafar.

3. Jia looked out the hotel window. The streets of New York were very different from the streets of the small town where she lived. She wanted to explore the city.

   A   Jia will go for a walk along the busy streets of New York.

   B   Jia will write postcards to her friends telling them about New York.

   C   Jia will read a book about living in New York City.

   D   Jia will go back to her small town.

4. Bomani needed a new car. He could only afford a used car. He was in a hurry, and he bought a car with dents. Much of the paint was scraped off. When Bomani started the engine, it made a coughing noise, and the car began to shake.

   F   Bomani will realize that this was the best purchase he had ever made.

   G   Bomani will decide to buy new tires for his car.

   H   Bomani will realize that the car will probably break down in a short while.

   J   Bomani will decide to show off his new car to his friends.

5. Miguel looked out the window. Dark clouds were gathering in the north. Soon the clouds covered the sun, and the wind began to blow. Just then Miguel remembered that he had left his book out on the patio.

   A   Miguel will play a video game with a friend.

   B   Miguel will go out to the patio to get his book.

   C   Miguel will go to the library to get another book.

   D   Miguel will close the window.

Use clues from the passage and what you already know to make predictions.

> Ebo smiled. How did his grandfather know he needed a new watch? It was the same watch that Ebo had admired at the mall. Ebo proudly wore his new watch every day. Saturday morning, he raked the yard. Later in the day, Ebo noticed his watch was missing.

1. Predict what will happen next.

_____

_____

> Diego measured the flour, sugar, salt, yeast, and water. He kneaded the dough and put it into a bread pan. He let the dough rise. Then he put the pan in the oven but forgot to set the timer. Later he saw smoke coming from the kitchen.

2. What do you predict the outcome will be?

_____

_____

> Mr. Lee was traveling to a small town. He studied a road map before he left. However, he didn't know that there had been a big snowstorm in the town the day before. When Mr. Lee got to the town, the signs were covered with snow.

3. What do you predict the outcome will be? _____

_____

> Tonya's cat, Evie, loves to eat tuna fish. Tonya began to make lunch. She opened a can of tuna fish and set it on the table. Just then the doorbell rang, and Tonya left the kitchen to answer the door.

4. Predict what will happen next.

_____

_____

Read each passage. Then circle the letter of the answer to each question.

> Hector took a pan of muffins out of the oven. He said to his brother, "Have a muffin when they have cooled, Julio." As soon as Hector left the kitchen, Julio grabbed a muffin.

1. What do you predict will happen next?

   A   Hector will make more muffins.

   B   Julio will burn his fingers.

   C   Julio will wash the muffin pan.

   D   Julio will pour himself a glass of milk.

> Mako enjoyed his woodworking class. He spent hours carving small wooden animals. His teacher said Mako was one of the best students he had. When the art festival came, Mako entered two of his best carvings.

2. What do you predict will happen next?

   F   Mako will win a ribbon at the art festival.

   G   Mako will decide to learn to paint.

   H   The judge won't like Mako's carved animals.

   J   Mako's teacher will win a ribbon at the art festival.

> Nasiha was taking a three-week trip to the East Coast. She had asked a neighbor to water her plants while she was away. As Nasiha boarded the plane to come home, she felt her house keys in the bottom of her purse. She had forgotten to give her neighbor her keys.

3. What do you predict the outcome will be?

   A   Nasiha's plants will be healthy when she returns.

   B   Nasiha will decide to drive home instead of fly.

   C   Nasiha's plants will be wilted from lack of water.

   D   Nasiha will not be able to get into her house when she returns.

Workplace Skill: Predict Outcomes from Employee Guidelines

An employee handbook provides guidelines for employees. As you read the handbook section below, make predictions about what will happen if an employee takes certain actions.

Read this section of an employee handbook. Then circle the letter of the answer to each question below the box.

Employee Handbook

Section 9: What You Can Do to Prevent Infections at Work

Germs are everywhere. Most of the time, they don't make us sick. However, sometimes they do. There are simple things you can do in the workplace to prevent germs from spreading. Here are a few measures our company requests you take to stay healthy.

- **Keep your hands clean.**
  Washing your hands regularly is the most important thing you can do. Make sure you always wash your hands after using the restroom.

- **Cover your mouth and nose when you cough or sneeze.**
  Always cough or sneeze into a clean tissue. Make sure to wash your hands afterward to prevent spreading germs to others. Sometimes, it is hard to get to a sink right away. Keep hand sanitizer at your workspace. If you are seriously ill, do not come to work. See Section 10 of the employee handbook for the company's sick-leave policy.

- **Practice good hygiene at your workspace.**
  Make sure to clean the surfaces of your workspace and the personal equipment you use daily with antibacterial wipes. Wipe your phone, your mouse, and your keyboard.

- **Take care of cuts, scratches, and wounds.**
  Your skin is your armor against harmful germs. Keep all cuts, scratches, and wounds clean and protected with a clean, dry bandage.

1. What do you predict will happen if you remember to wash your hands frequently?

   A The personal equipment you use will remain dirty.

   B You will avoid getting cuts, scratches, and wounds.

   C You will be less likely to spread germs to your coworkers.

   D You will not need bandages if you get a cut.

2. The coworker next to you has a cold and is not covering her mouth when she coughs. What do you predict will happen?

   F You will not get the cold.

   G Your department will shut down for a week.

   H Your coworker will pass the cold on to others.

   J Your supervisor will request that both of you stay home.

Write for Work

Suppose that you work for a company that is creating a page for the employee handbook. The company wants to create a policy for personal cell-phone usage at work. They have asked for employee input and suggestions. In a notebook write an e-mail or a letter to your manager with your suggestions. Think about when and how using personal cell phones in the workplace would be acceptable. Think about when and how using personal cell phones would not be acceptable.

  Reading Extension

Turn to "Journey to Saturn" on page 73 of *Reading Basics Introductory Reader*. After you have read and/or listened to the article, answer the questions below.

Circle the letter of the answer to each question.

1. What clues does the author give that the scientists would find ice in Saturn's rings?

   A Humans have known about Saturn for thousands of years.

   B More than 750 Earths could fit inside Saturn if it were hollow.

   C Saturn is so light that it could float in water.

   D Scientists knew the rings were cold.

2. Paragraph 10 describes the powerful cameras on the spacecraft. What do you think will happen with these cameras?

   F Scientists will not study the pictures.

   G Scientists will learn more about Saturn.

   H Scientists will wait until they have more powerful cameras.

   J Scientists will never use the cameras.

Write the answer to each question.

3. Reread paragraphs 1 through 4. What did you predict was going to happen while you were reading?

   _____

   _____

4. Write the clues from the text or from your own knowledge that you used to make the prediction in item 3.

   _____

   _____

5. Explain the prediction that a spacecraft will never be able to land on Saturn.

   _____

   _____

Explore Words

VOWEL COMBINATIONS

Two vowels can come together to stand for one vowel sound. The vowel pairs *ai* and *ay* stand for the long *a* sound as in *play* and *paint*. The vowel pair *ee* stands for the long *e* sound as in *seed*. The letters *ea* can stand for the long *e* sound as in *eat*, or the short *e* sound as in *sweat*.

In items 1–4, circle the word that has the long *a* sound. In items 5–8, circle the word that has the long *e* sound.

1. Esteban and Hamid sat down to (deal, play) cards.
2. The sweater was a dark (gray, teal) color.
3. My dog's (ear, tail) is black.
4. Manu did not feel (pain, free).

5. Ellen got scared and (fainted, screamed).
6. Paloma rode in a (jeep, train) to New York.
7. They walked along the (beach, bay).
8. They tried to (keep, bail) the water out of the boat.

CONSONANT PAIRS *wr, kn, gn*

Each of these consonant pairs stands for only one sound—the sound of the second letter: *wr, kn, gn*. The first letter in each pair is silent.

Write *wr, kn,* or *gn* to complete the word in each sentence.

1. Bao forgot to si_____ the check.
2. The yarn had a big _____ot in it.
3. Nico _____ashes her teeth while she sleeps.

4. Chelsea bought the _____ong brand of detergent.
5. Panya used a _____ife to carve the turkey.
6. It took a long time to _____ing out all the wet laundry.

SYNONYMS

Synonyms are words that have the same or about the same meaning. *Kind* and *caring* are synonyms. Their meanings are similar.

Write the word from the box that is a synonym for each numbered word.

greet	clean	peel	sweet	scrape	wreck

1. spotless _____
2. sugary _____
3. welcome _____

4. ruin _____
5. scratch _____
6. skin _____

SPELLING: POSSESSIVES

Use an apostrophe and the letter *s* to show possession. Write the apostrophe before the *s* (*'s*) if only one person possesses the item. The phrase *the boy's hats* mean that the hats belong to one boy. Write the apostrophe after the *s* (*s'*) to show that more than one person possesses something. The phrase *the boys' hats* mean that the hats belong to more than one boy.

Rewrite each phrase using the singular possessive form. The first one has been done for you.

1. the book that Jason owns _____*Jason's book*_____

2. the toy that the cat has _____

3. the skirt belonging to the woman _____

4. the feathers on one duck _____

Rewrite each phrase using the plural possessive form.

5. the bats of many players _____

6. the computers of several workers _____

7. the rules of all teachers _____

8. the needs that parents have _____

ACADEMIC VOCABULARY

Knowing these high-frequency words will help you in many school subjects.

predict   to make a guess about something that will happen based on clues

prior   previous

outcome   result

adjust   to change

logical   clearly and soundly reasoned

Complete the sentences below using one of the words above.

1. What was the _____ of the tennis match?

2. The student could answer the question because of his _____ knowledge.

3. Sheila needed to _____ the picture that was hanging crookedly.

4. Can you _____ what will happen tomorrow?

5. Ping looked at all of the facts carefully and came to a _____ conclusion.

Lesson 2.6

Read Maps

A map shows where places are located. There are different kinds of maps. A physical map shows different features of an area. These can include mountains, deserts, and rivers. Other maps use colors, patterns, and symbols to represent information. Maps are usually drawn to scale. The scale beneath this map shows that one inch is equal to four miles. The scale shows how far places on the map are from each other. Using a ruler, you can figure out that the fire station is three miles from the police station.

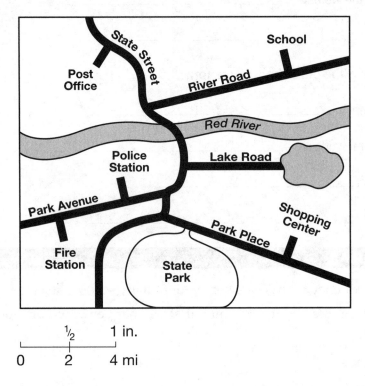

Use the map to figure out about how many miles the entrance of the state park is from the entrance of the shopping center.

Find the state park. Then look at the road that goes by it: Park Place. Next, measure from the entrance of the state park to the entrance of shopping center. You can use a ruler or mark an inch on a scrap of paper. The shopping center entrance is about one inch from the state park entrance. The scale tells you that one inch means four miles in real distance.

Most maps include a key or legend. The key tells what the symbols on the map represent. The letters on the side of the map and the numbers across the top are called coordinates. Coordinates give the location of a specific place. Coordinates help you easily find what you are looking for on the map. Look for the Dolphin Show in A2.

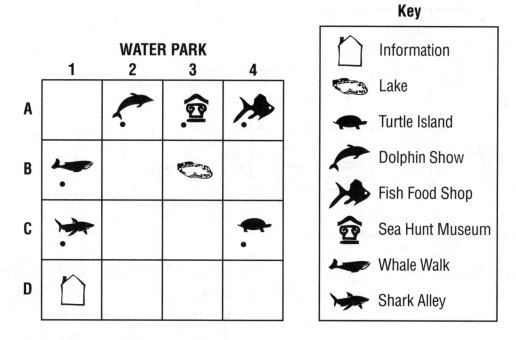

Use the coordinate grid and the key to answer the questions.

1. What does the symbol ⌂ represent? _____

2. What does the symbol 🐠 represent? _____

3. What does the symbol 🐬 represent? _____

4. Which place is farthest from Information? _____

5. In what row is the Sea Hunt Museum? _____

6. In what column is the Whale Walk? _____

7. Write the coordinates for the lake. _____

8. Write the coordinates for the Sea Hunt Museum. _____

9. What is located at coordinates C1? _____

10. What is located at coordinates C4? _____

Ridgeville

	1	2	3	4	5
A	Book store •	Library •	Restaurant •		Theater •
B	• State house	• Monument			Statue •
C	Parking lot •			City park •	
D	Doctor's office •	Office building •	• Grocery store	• Clothing store	Apartment house •

feet 0 25 50 75 100

inches 0   ½   1

Circle the letter of the answer to each question.

1. What is located at coordinate B5?

   A state house

   B office building

   C monument

   D statue

2. What are the coordinates for the grocery store?

   F D3

   G C4

   H D4

   J A1

3. What is the distance from the statue to the monument?

   A about 25 feet

   B about 50 feet

   C about 200 feet

   D about 350 feet

4. About how far is it from the parking lot to the grocery store?

   F about 2 feet

   G about 75 feet

   H about 150 feet

   J about 200 feet

5. What are the coordinates for the monument?

   A B2

   B C3

   C A5

   D B5

6. What is located at coordinate C4?

   F doctor's office

   G parking Lot

   H city park

   J clothing store

7. What is closest in distance to the theater?

   A statue

   B restaurant

   C city park

   D monument

8. Which of these places is farthest away from the office building?

   F doctor's office

   G grocery store

   H library

   J parking lot

Read the map. Write the answer to each question.

MONTANA

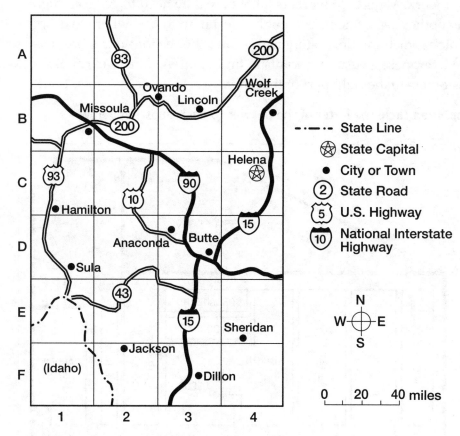

1. What is the capital of Montana? _____

2. What kind of road is 83? _____

3. What kind of road is 15? _____

4. About how far is Sula from the Idaho border? _____

5. About how far is it by road from Butte to Wolf Creek? _____

6. What are the coordinates for Sheridan? _____

7. What three roads are in coordinate B2? _____

8. Write the city located at each of these coordinates.

C1 _____   B1 _____   C4 _____

E4 _____   F2 _____   B4 _____

Workplace Skill: Read a Store Map

People use maps at work. Maps help workers get where they need to go. You might use a map to find another department. You might use a map to find where to drop something off or pick something up. A store map shows the sections of a store. The sections are labeled. Suppose a customer wants to find paint. A store map can help workers point customers to the right part of the store.

Read the store map. Then circle the letter of the answer to each question below.

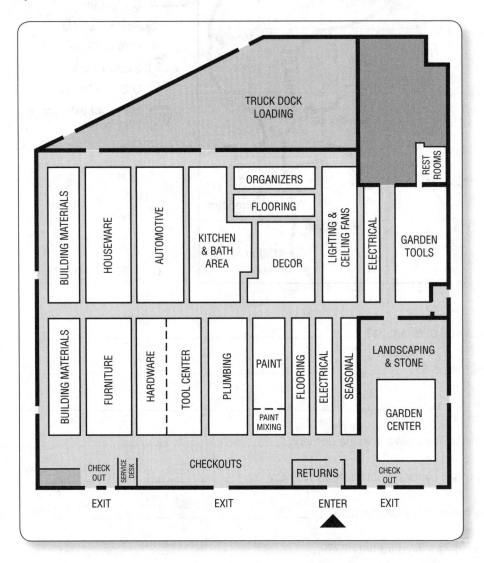

1. Checkouts are located closest to the

A   entrance.

B   exits.

C   garden center.

D   tool center.

2. The restrooms are located next to the

F   flooring department.

G   doors and windows department.

H   garden tools department.

J   checkout counters.

Write for Work

Imagine that you work in the returns department of the store that is mapped on page 122. A customer wants to know where ceiling fans are located. In a notebook, write the directions for the customer.

Workplace Extension

Company Dress Code

Chantal is an administrative assistant at her company. She knows the company's dress-code rules. The rules are included in the employee handbook. The rules state that on Monday through Thursday, the attire is business casual. People should dress in a neat, businesslike fashion. She knows that "trendy" fashions are not considered professional. Employees have to use common sense. For casual Fridays, jeans, sandals, and sneakers are fine. Shorts and flip-flops are not.

Chantal has a new coworker, Sharon, working next to her. She noticed that during her first week at work, Sharon often wore jeans and a T-shirt. On casual Friday, she wore shorts to work. Chantal wants to help her coworker, but she still wants to remain on friendly terms. She wonders what to do.

Circle the letter of the answer to each question.

1. What type of dress should *not* be worn Monday through Thursday?

   A a shirt and trousers

   B a business suit

   C jeans or T-shirts

   D a skirt and jacket

2. "Business casual" means you should wear

   F trendy fashions.

   G sandals.

   H jeans.

   J neat business attire.

Write the answer to each question.

3. Why might a company have a dress code policy?

   _____

4. How might Chantal tell Sharon about the company's dress code policy?

   _____

   _____

Explore Words

VOWEL COMBINATIONS

Two vowels can come together to stand for one vowel sound. The vowel pairs *oa* and *oe* stand for the long *o* sound in *toast* and *foe*. The vowel *o* also combines with *w* to stand for the long *o* sound, as in *throw*. Vowel pairs stand for the long *i* sound in *tie* and for the long *u* sound in *argue*.

Read the sentences. Write the vowel combination that completes each word.

1. Please open the wind_____ to let in some air. (ay, ow)

2. When the baby cr_____s, you need to pick her up. (ie, ue)

3. What did the doctor say about your sore thr_____t? (ue, oa)

4. Bring these books back to the library when they are d_____. (ow, ue)

5. Rosa will take a bus when she g_____s to Arizona. (ai, oe)

r-CONTROLLED VOWELS

When the letter *r* follows a vowel, it changes the sound that the vowel represents. You can hear the difference in these word pairs: *cat / car, spot / sport, stove / store*.

Circle the word that has the *r*-controlled vowel sound to complete each sentence.

1. Use a red pencil to (make, mark) your changes.

2. Javier saved his change in an empty (jar, can).

3. Ahmed is very (small, smart) for his age.

4. Take a left at the next (corner, stoplight).

5. My old coat looks very (shabby, worn).

6. I hope this cut doesn't leave a (scar, scab).

ANTONYMS

Antonyms are words that have opposite or almost opposite meanings. For example, *safe* and *dangerous* are antonyms.

Write an antonym for each underlined word.

1. Writing my report was difficult. _____

2. The huge moth flew through the window. _____

3. Did you remember to pick up milk? _____

4. I feel weak when I work out. _____

5. The actor enters from the left side of the stage. _____

Homophones are words that sound the same but are spelled differently and have different meanings. For example, each of these pairs of words are homophones: *ad / add, close / clothes.*

Circle the two words in each row that are homophones. The first item has already been done for you.

1. (bee)	bees	best	(be)
2. knee	no	knew	new
3. know	knows	now	nose
4. two	toes	too	tow
5. flood	floor	flower	flour
6. sun	soon	son	seen
7. at	night	eight	ate
8. blow	blew	blue	flow
9. peel	pail	pal	pale
10. wood	wad	wade	would
11. seal	see	sail	sea
12. tile	tall	tale	tail

ACADEMIC VOCABULARY

Knowing these academic words will help you in many school subjects.

key   a list of symbols used in a map and their meanings

physical   having to do with nature or natural things

feature   a distinctive part of a thing

symbol   a mark, sign, or picture that stands for something else

area   a region

Complete the sentences below using one of the words above.

1. She checked the whole _____ and did not find her lost wallet.

2. He needed to know about the mountains and rivers in a city, so he used a _____ map.

3. The _____ shows that capital cities are marked with stars.

4. The _____ for an ATM is a dollar sign.

5. Which _____ do you think is the most important for using a map correctly?

Unit 2 Review

Find the Main Idea

A paragraph is a group of sentences. The main idea is what the paragraph is about. It may be stated or implied. The main idea links all the details together.

Identify Cause and Effect

You ask *why* when you want to know the cause of something. When you read, you may learn about some things that make other things happen. The event that happens is the effect. The reason it happens is the cause. Some words that signal cause and effect are *so, therefore*, and *because*.

Use Consumer Materials

We are all consumers of products and services. When we buy products, we need to know important information about them in order to use them safely. Labels on packages, advertisements, and company policies are examples of consumer materials.

Identify Fact and Opinion

Facts are statements that can be proved. You can look them up or check them in some way. Opinions are statements that tell what someone believes or thinks. When you read, it is important to separate facts from opinions.

Predict Outcomes

When you read, clues in the story can help you figure out what might happen next. You notice details in the story and then think about your own experiences. You can use this information to predict an outcome.

Read Maps

A map is a kind of picture that shows where places are located. There are many different kinds of maps. Most maps include a key or legend that explains any symbols on the map. Many maps use a scale to show distance.

Unit 2 Assessment

Read each passage. Then circle the letter of the answer to each question.

> *Earth* is a stupid name for our planet. The word *earth* means "land." However, our planet's surface is more than 70 percent water. Earth is unique among the planets in the solar system. It is the only one to have oceans. Earth's five oceans are named the Pacific, the Atlantic, the Indian, the Southern, and the Arctic.

1. Which sentence states an opinion?

   A Earth is a stupid name for our planet.

   B The word *earth* means "land."

   C Earth is unique among the planets in the solar system.

   D It is the only one to have oceans.

2. Which sentence states the main idea of the passage?

   F *Earth* is the perfect name for our planet.

   G Earth has more water than land.

   H Earth is a unique planet.

   J The Pacific is the largest ocean.

> Shani looked outside after the snow stopped. There were a few hoof tracks in the yard. The tracks gave Shani an idea for a joke. She put on just one boot. Then she hopped around the yard, leaving tracks in a circle. She knew that her brother would be home in three hours. He would wonder what animal had made those strange tracks. When Shani got back inside, it started to snow again, even harder.

3. What is the main idea of this passage?

   A Shani looked outside after the snow stopped.

   B Shani wanted to play a joke on her brother.

   C There were hoof tracks in the yard.

   D She put on just one boot.

4. What do you predict will happen when Shani's brother gets home?

   F Her brother will make tracks in the snow.

   G A strange animal will appear in the yard.

   H The snow will be covering Shani's tracks, ruining the joke.

   J Her brother will be frightened because of the strange tracks.

5. The tracks Shani saw in the snow were probably made by

   A a car.

   B an elephant.

   C a sled.

   D a deer.

6. Which of the following statements is an opinion?

   F Shani's idea for a joke was silly.

   G Shani got an idea for a joke.

   H It started to snow again.

   J Shani left tracks in a circle.

You may think that all lions look alike. This is not true. You can tell lions apart by their whiskers. The whiskers grow in tufts. The holes that their whiskers grow out of are grouped in patterns. Only an animal trainer should get close enough to see the difference!

7. Which statement is not a fact?

A You can tell lions apart by their whiskers.

B Lions' whiskers grow in tufts.

C The holes that their whiskers grow out of are grouped in patterns.

D Only an animal trainer should get close enough to see the difference!

8. Based on what you read in the passage, which statement is factual?

F You can tell lions apart by the color of their whiskers.

G On each lion, the groups of whiskers are arranged in a different pattern.

H There is no way to tell lions apart.

J All lions look exactly alike.

Community Announcement
Looking for Volunteers

The local chapter of Support the Boys and Girls Club is looking for new adult helpers. We are all volunteers. There are many ways to help the children. Can you tutor after school? Can you coach a sport? The state has cut the program budget for the Boys and Girls Club. Without help from the community, this valuable resource for our children will not survive. Please join us any Monday afternoon for the weekly orientation session. The need for new members has never been greater. We look forward to meeting you!

9. What is the main idea of this announcement?

A We are all volunteers.

B The state has cut the program budget for the Boys and Girls Club.

C We look forward to meeting you.

D The local chapter of Support the Boys and Girls Club needs new members.

10. What will be the effect if people do not volunteer to help?

F The Boys and Girls Club will have to close.

G The volunteers will leave the community.

H The orientation session will move to Friday morning.

J The program budget will be increased by the state.

Study the map. Then circle the letter of the answer to each question.

Distances Between Major U.S. Cities
(in miles)

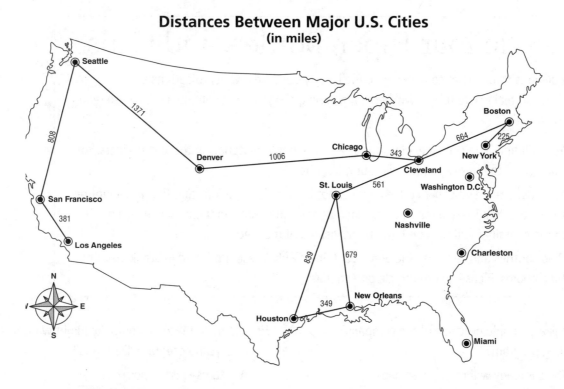

11. Of the following cities, which two are the closest to each other?

A Chicago and Denver

B Boston and New York

C San Francisco and Los Angeles

D Houston and New Orleans

12. What direction would you travel to drive from Denver to Seattle?

F northeast

G northwest

H southeast

J southwest

13. If you travel 400 miles a day, about how many days should you allow to go from Denver to Seattle?

A two days

B three days

C four days

D five days

14. According to this map, which two cities are between 500 and 600 miles apart?

F Seattle and San Francisco

G St. Louis and Cleveland

H New York and Boston

J Houston and Cleveland

15. In what direction would you travel to get to Chicago from Denver?

A north

B south

C east

D west

16. Which of these pairs of cities is farthest apart?

F Cleveland and Boston

G Denver and Seattle

H New York and Boston

J Los Angeles and San Francisco

Read the announcement. Then circle the letter of the answer to each question.

Recycle Your Paper, Bottles, and Cans

Office buildings throw away tons of paper. The Liberty Company wants to curb its waste.
No one likes to feel wasteful! We will begin a recycling program on September 1st. Please read about the details:

- You will find blue containers by your desk. Place paper materials in these containers. You don't need to remove staples, clips, or rubber bands.
- Food wrappers and paper coffee cups cannot be recycled. Napkins and tissues cannot be recycled either. These items will contaminate the other items in the container. Everything in the container will then be thrown out instead of recycled.
- Place bottles and cans into the green containers only. These are found in break areas or lunchrooms. Please do not recycle broken glass.

17. What is a probable outcome of the company's recycling program?

    A The company will recycle less paper.

    B The company will produce less waste.

    C The company will use fewer napkins.

    D The company will need more containers.

18. What is an effect of throwing a napkin in a blue trash container?

    F The napkin and the other items in the container will be thrown out as trash.

    G The napkin will be moved to a brown trash container.

    H The other items in the container will be recycled, and the napkin will be thrown away as trash.

    J The napkin and the other items in the container will be recycled.

19. The main reason a company might want to start a recycling program like this is

    A to use less paper.

    B to gain more employees.

    C to be more environmentally responsible.

    D to buy more paper.

20. Which sentence from the announcement expresses an opinion?

    F Food wrappers and paper coffee cups cannot be recycled.

    G We will begin a recycling program on September 1st.

    H No one likes to feel wasteful!

    J The Liberty Company wants to curb its waste.

Read the memo. Then circle the letter of the answer to each question.

From: Office Manager
To: Summer Employees of the J. Wilkey Company
Subject: Office Supplies

Thank you all for attending yesterday's meeting. The meeting was about office supplies at the J. Wilkey Company. See the summary list below.

- We keep regular office supplies in the copy machine room. This room is in Hall 3.
- You will find pencils, pens, binder clips, and sticky notes in the bins.
- You will find copy paper and folders on the shelves.
- Please take only the supplies you need.
- If you need something, ask Kerry James who orders the office supplies.
- Please mark the inventory sheet if you take the next-to-last item. See the sample sheet below.

Office Supplies Inventory Sheet
July
Please note below when you take the next-to-last item, box, or package.

Office Supply	Date Taken	Employee Name
Mechanical pencils	July 23	Emelita Suarez
Erasable pens		
Copy paper		
Folders	July 12	James Buckley
Binder clips		

21. What is the main idea of this memo?

A Office supplies can be found near the copy machine.

B Summer employees need to ask Kerry James for office supplies.

C Summer employees need to know about office supplies.

D Kerry James orders all the office supplies.

22. Which supplies are not considered regular?

F staplers and paper punchers

G pens and pencils

H copy paper and folders

J binder clips

23. What can employees do to help track office supplies?

A They can go to the copy room at different times of day.

B They can mark the inventory sheet in the copy room.

C They can use both sides of each sheet of paper.

D They can choose pens instead of pencils.

24. What could be the effect if people take more supplies than they need?

F Kerry James may no longer be the receptionist.

G Employees may have to come to another meeting.

H The company might not allow employees to take their own supplies.

J Office supplies might be moved to Hall 4.

Circle the letter of the answer to each question.

25. In which word does *y* make the long *e* sound?

   A   sky

   B   silly

   C   reply

   D   bay

26. Which word is the plural of *wish*?

   F   wish

   G   wishs

   H   wishes

   J   wishis

27. Which word is a synonym for *strong*?

   A   string

   B   style

   C   weak

   D   powerful

28. Which word fits into both sentences?

We saw a _____ of lions in a nature movie.

Welders take great _____ in their work.

   F   group

   G   pride

   H   place

   J   care

29. Which phrase means *the laptop belonging to Sue*?

   A   Sue's laptop

   B   Sue laptop

   C   Sues' laptop

   D   Sues laptop

30. Which is the correct meaning of *misfile*?

   F   file incorrectly

   G   file late

   H   file before

   J   file under

31. Which word has a silent consonant?

   A   write

   B   real

   C   burn

   D   grin

32. Which word correctly completes the sentence?

Janayah did well on the test because she was _____ and checked all her answers.

   F   caring

   G   careless

   H   creative

   J   careful

33. Which word does not have the long *a* sound?

   A   braid

   B   lake

   C   stand

   D   delay

34. Which pair of words are homophones?

   F   no, know

   G   brand, band

   H   grim, grime

   J   brand, strand

35. In which word does the letter *c* stand for the soft *c* sound?

   A   canteen

   B   recall

   C   celery

   D   camper

36. In which word does the letter *g* stand for the hard *g* sound?

   F   germ

   G   gallop

   H   cage

   J   danger

Unit 3

In this unit you will learn how to

You will practice the following workplace skills

You will also learn new words and their meanings and put your reading skills to work in written activities. You will get additional reading practice in *Reading Basics Introductory Reader*.

Lesson 3.1

Identify Sequence

Sequence is the order in which things are connected or events take place. Putting things or events in sequence can be used for many purposes.

Purpose	Example
To explain how something works	How an electric switch works
To explain steps in a process	How to make pizza
To describe a routine	How you get ready in the morning
To tell about an event or experience	A funny thing that happened on the first day of your job

This time order, or sequence, helps the reader understand how events, concepts, and themes relate to one another. Information is often presented in the order in which events happened. Look for words that signal time order, such as *first, before, next, after, last, finally,* and *then.* Read this example:

> First, Manjira found her library card. Next, she walked to the library. Then she returned her books. After that, she browsed through the stacks for some new novels. Finally, she checked out her books and headed home.

In the example above, the writer has used signal words to tell the reader in what order things happened. When sequence is used to give directions, the writer may use signal words or number each step. Read the instructions for using a fax machine:

1. Press *hook.*
2. Dial 9, 1, and the fax number with area code.
3. Put document facedown in feeder tray.
4. When you hear a fax tone, press *fax start.*

Read the paragraph and underline the signal words.

> You can make whipped cream from heavy cream. First, chill a metal bowl. Then put heavy cream in the bowl. Add sugar and vanilla. Next, beat the cream with an electric mixer. Finally, beat until soft peaks form.

Did you underline *first, then, next,* and *finally*? These are all words that the writer uses to help you understand the order of events.

Read the passages about the process of making something. In the exercises, the steps are listed in incorrect order. Write numbers on the lines to show the correct order of the steps.

Maple syrup is made from the sap of maple trees. The sap is collected during the sugaring season, or early spring. In the traditional method, farmers bore a hole in the maple tree trunk. Then, they put a metal or wooden spout in the hole. They hang a bucket from the spout. Sap drips from the spout into the bucket. Once a day the farmers collect the sap. They boil it. The water boils away. Maple syrup is left.

---

1. A The farmers boil the sap. _____

   B The farmers put a hole in the tree. _____

   C Sap drips from the spout. _____

   D The farmers put a spout in the hole. _____

   E The farmers hang a bucket from the tree. _____

In 1863 the world's first subway opened in London, England. First, workers dug up the road. Then, they dug a deep ditch. Then, they laid tracks in the ditch. Next, they built brick arches over the tracks. Finally, they laid a new road over the arches.

---

2. A Workers laid tracks in the ditch. _____

   B Workers dug up the road. _____

   C Workers laid a new road on top. _____

   D Workers dug a deep ditch. _____

   E Workers built brick arches over the tracks. _____

A grilled cheese sandwich is easy to make. First, put a skillet on a hot burner. Next, assemble two pieces of buttered bread and some cheese. Then, place the sandwich in the skillet. Finally, flip the sandwich to cook the other side.

---

3. A Flip the sandwich. _____

   B Put a skillet on a hot burner. _____

   C Put the sandwich in the skillet. _____

   D Assemble the sandwich. _____

Read the passage. Then fill out the graphic organizer with the steps of a dust devil's formation in the order they occur.

Dust devils are a type of whirlwind that appears in deserts all over the world. They get started on hot, dry days. First, the sand gets very hot from the sun. The hot sand heats the air directly above it. Because heat rises, the air closest to the ground may rush upward. This rush of air pulls more air behind it. It pulls hot sand from the ground. Air currents wrap around the rising air and spin around it. The whirlwind has a cone shape. In the end, it spins across the desert.

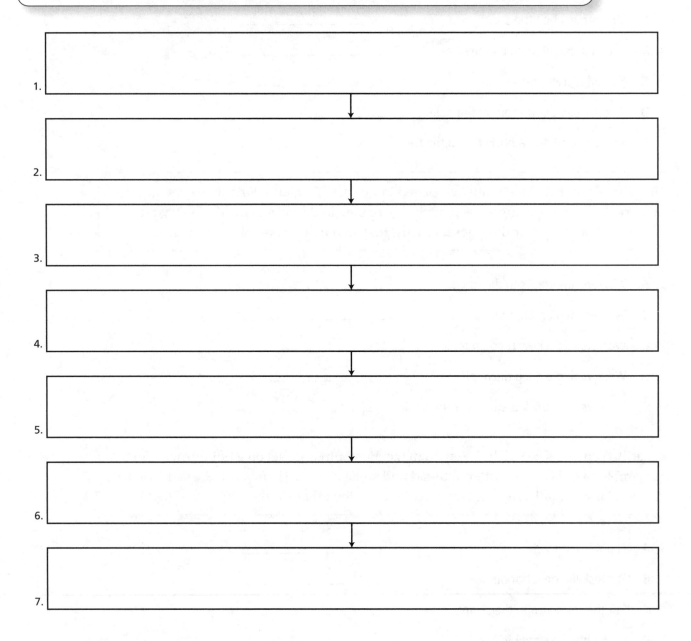

1.

2.

3.

4.

5.

6.

7.

Read the passage. Then circle the letter of the answer to each question.

Ancient Greek myths say that the first echo came from a beautiful young maiden named Echo. Echo had only one fault. She talked too much. The Greek god Zeus used Echo to distract his wife, Hera. Echo chatted idly to Hera while Zeus chased nymphs. When Hera found out that Echo had helped Zeus, she punished Echo. After that, Echo could never speak on her own. All she could do was repeat the words of others. Later, Echo fell in love with a handsome young man named Narcissus, but the young man did not love Echo. He loved only himself. Echo became so sad that she faded away until all that was left of her was her voice.

1. What happened after Hera found out that Echo had helped trick her?

   A   Hera chatted idly with Echo.

   B   Zeus chased nymphs.

   C   Echo had the fault of talking too much.

   D   Hera punished Echo.

2. What happened before Echo fell in love with Narcissus?

   F   Echo lost the ability to speak on her own.

   G   Narcissus did not love her.

   H   Echo faded away.

   J   All that was left of Echo was her voice.

3. When did Echo lose the ability to speak for herself?

   A   at the same time that she fell in love with Narcissus

   B   after she became very sad

   C   before Zeus chased nymphs

   D   after Hera punished her

4. What happened at the same time Echo distracted Hera?

   F   Echo faded away.

   G   Zeus chased nymphs.

   H   Echo fell in love with Narcissus.

   J   Hera punished Echo in anger.

5. When did Echo fade away?

   A   after she became sad

   B   as she chatted idly to Hera

   C   before she fell in love with Narcissus

   D   while Zeus chased nymphs

6. When did Hera find out that Echo had helped Zeus?

   F   after Echo stopped speaking on her own

   G   after Zeus chased nymphs

   H   after Echo faded away

   J   after Echo fell in love with Narcissus

Workplace Skill: Recognize Sequence in a Safety Procedure

Companies establish workplace safety procedures to protect their employees and the workplace environment. Procedures are written steps for completing an activity. When you read a sequence of steps in a procedure, look for words that show the order of events.

Read the procedure. Then circle the letter of the answer to each question below the box.

Factory Safety Procedure
Using a Fire Extinguisher

Knowing how to use a fire extinguisher in the workplace is important. It's possible for small fires to start near metal grinding machines. There are three fire extinguishers in our factory. One is near the entrance, one is near the foreman's office, and one is located in the lunch room. It is important to remember that the fire extinguisher should only be used for small fires. Familiarize yourself with the procedures in the Employee Handbook in case of a large fire.

Remember this acronym: **P.A.S.S.** (Pull, Aim, Squeeze, Sweep).

Pull: First, find the pin at the top of the extinguisher. Pull it out to unlock the fire extinguisher.

Aim: Next, aim the fire extinguisher at the base of the fire. Many people want to spray directly at the flames. However, if you do this, the fire will not go out. The spray will go right through the fire. Aiming at the base of the fire will help you hit the fuel of the fire and put the fire out.

Squeeze: Then squeeze the handle to release the chemicals in the extinguisher. The chemicals will put out the fire.

Sweep: Finally, sweep the extinguisher from side to side across the base of the fire until the fire is out. Start by standing at a safe distance from the fire. Gradually move forward. Once the fire is out, do not walk away from the fire. Fires can reignite, or restart. After you use the fire extinguisher, make sure you let the foreman know that it needs to be recharged.

---

1. What should you do after you pull the pin on the fire extinguisher?

   A   Consult the Employee Handbook.

   B   Aim the fire extinguisher at the base of the fire.

   C   Sweep the extinguisher from side to side.

   D   Locate where the fire extinguishers are placed.

2. What step is important to remember after using the fire extinguisher?

   F   Let the foreman know that the fire extinguisher needs to be recharged.

   G   Remember the acronym P.A.S.S.

   H   Pull the pin on the fire extinguisher.

   J   Squeeze the handle.

Write for Work

You will often need to follow a sequence of steps in the workplace. It is helpful to put each step in your own words. This helps you understand the correct sequence. You may find it helpful to keep track of the steps by making a numbered list. Read the instructions for using a fire extinguisher. In a notebook, write a numbered list of the sequence of steps for using a fire extinguisher in your own words.

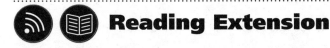 **Reading Extension**

Turn to "Separate Lives" on page 81 of *Reading Basics Introductory Reader*. After you have read and/or listened to the article, answer the questions below.

Circle the letter of the answer to each question.

1. What happened after the doctors pinched off the twins' vein in their hearts?

   A The doctors separated the rib cages.

   B The twins had to travel to a hospital in Maryland.

   C The hearts kept beating.

   D The doctors separated the livers.

2. At what point during pregnancy do twins become conjoined?

   F during birth

   G when the egg splits

   H before the egg splits

   J after birth

3. What was the first step in the process of separating the twins?

   A The doctors divided the girls' ribs.

   B The doctors separated the girls' liver.

   C The doctors separated the girls' hearts.

   D The doctors divided the large vein.

Write the answer to each question.

4. How did the doctors practice the surgery before the operation?

   _____

5. After what step in the operation did the doctors learn that the twins shared a large vein in the heart?

   _____

Explore Words

r-CONTROLLED VOWELS

When the letter *r* follows a vowel, it changes the usual sound of the vowel. For example, say *gem* and *germ*. The word *germ* has an *r*-controlled vowel sound.

Say each word in parentheses aloud. Complete the sentences with words that have the *r*-controlled vowel sound. Circle the word.

1. Mike is making (turkey, chicken) for dinner.
2. Juliana left her (notebook, purse) on the table.
3. Niko hopes to get into (nursing, law) school.
4. Joe has to write a 500-(word, page) essay.
5. You will soon (drive, merge) onto the highway.
6. Let me know when you get (hungry, thirsty).

LETTERS *x* AND *qu*

The letter *x* can stand for the sound of *ks*, as in the word *box*. The letter *x* can also stand for the sound of *gz*, as in *exit*. The *gz* sound is usually—but not always—heard when the letter *x* comes between two vowels. The letters *qu* can stand for the *kw* sound, as in *quiet*. They also can sound like the letter *k*, as in *antique*.

Say each word or ask your teacher to say it. Write *ks* or *gz* on the line to indicate the sound of the letter *x* in a word. Write *kw* or *k* on the line to indicate the sound of the letters *qu* in a word.

1. exam _____
2. relax _____
3. request _____
4. technique _____

CONTEXT CLUES

When you read, you can use context to help you figure out the meaning of an unfamiliar word. Context is the surrounding words, phrases, and sentences that give you clues to the word's meaning.

Use context clues in each sentence to figure out the meaning of each underlined word. Write the meaning on the line.

1. Bentley wanted a yacht, but he bought a smaller boat. _____

2. I loathe spiders, and I hate snakes too. _____

3. Mom tried to console the baby, but she could not comfort her. _____

4. Kwon said he was healthy, but he did not look robust. _____

5. We saw a spring peeper, a kind of tree frog. _____

SYNONYMS AND ANTONYMS

Synonyms are words that have the same or almost the same meanings. For example, *strong* and *powerful* are synonyms. **Antonyms** are words that have opposite or nearly opposite meanings. For example, *strong* and *weak* are antonyms.

Choose one word from the box that is a synonym and another word that is an antonym for each numbered word. Write the words on the lines.

real	worried	silly	tiny	flimsy
calm	huge	sturdy	serious	made up

	Synonym	**Antonym**
1. nervous	_____	_____
2. enormous	_____	_____
3. delicate	_____	_____
4. foolish	_____	_____
5. imaginary	_____	_____

ACADEMIC VOCABULARY

Knowing these high-frequency words will help you in many school subjects.

sequence   the order in which things are connected

purpose   the reason something is done

relate   to be connected

order   the arrangement of things in relation to each other according to a certain pattern

directions   instructions for going somewhere or doing something

Complete the sentences below using one of the words above.

1. Afra was disappointed that the book she bought did not _____ to her paper topic.

2. The _____ of the expedition was to find a new species of beetle.

3. Derrick needed _____ to get to the bus station, so he looked online.

4. The _____ of steps in the dance followed the music closely.

5. The librarian shelved the books in alphabetical _____.

Lesson 3.2

Compare and Contrast

When you think about how two or more things are alike and different, you are making comparisons and contrasts. Comparing tells how things are alike, while contrasting tells how things are different. Writers will often use comparison and contrast within the same passage. To compare and contrast, ask yourself, "How are these two people, places, or things alike? How are they different?"

Writers sometimes give clues to let readers know whether they are comparing or contrasting. The following words and phrases listed are some of the clue words that can be used.

Words That Show Comparison		Words That Show Contrast	
and	as	although	in contrast
both	likewise	however	but
like	in the same way	still	on the other hand

Read the example below. The writer is contrasting plants that people grow for their use with plants that people grow for their beauty. The phrase *on the other hand* is a signal the writer uses to tell readers that he or she is contrasting two things.

> Some people grow plants because the plants are useful. People make food, cloth, wood, and dyes from these plants. On the other hand, some people raise plants just because they are pretty to look at. People have enjoyed beautiful gardens since ancient times.

Read the passage. Underline the words that show that the writer is comparing. Circle the words that show that the writer is contrasting.

> In some ways, plants and animals are alike. They are both alive. They both grow. They both respond to light and water. It is easy to see that there are big differences, however. For example, animals respond more to the world around them than plants. Plants respond very slowly. Animals are not rooted to one spot. They can roam the fields and forests. They eat solid food. In contrast, plants are able to make their own food.

You should have underlined *alike* and *both*. You should have circled *differences*, *however*, and *in contrast*.

Read each passage. Then answer the questions.

> Both Jake's Grill and Chez Paris serve delicious food, but each restaurant serves a different kind of food. Jake's is the best barbecue in town. On the other hand, Chez Paris serves the best French food. At Jake's, the food is hot and spicy, and the servings are huge. In contrast, Chez Paris does not serve hot and spicy food. Also, the portions are small. In addition, the atmosphere at the two restaurants is different. Jake's is plain and simple, but the dining room at Chez Paris is elegant. The cost of meals is different too. Dinner at Jake's is cheap, but dinner at Chez Paris is expensive. Both restaurants offer wonderful dining experiences.

1. What two things does the passage compare and contrast?

_____

2. In what ways are the two restaurants alike?

_____

3. Which words and phrases signal differences between Chez Paris and Jake's Grill?

_____

> A kangaroo rat and a rat kangaroo are different animals. Both are about a foot long and hop on long back legs. Both have a head like a rat and a long tail. However, the kangaroo rat is a rodent and has some white fur. The rat kangaroo is a marsupial and is brown. Kangaroo rats don't drink water. They get the water they need from food. On the other hand, rat kangaroos do need to drink water. Kangaroo rats live only in North America, while rat kangaroos live in Australia. The biggest difference of all is that the rat kangaroo has a pouch, and the kangaroo rat does not.

4. What two things does the passage compare and contrast?

_____

5. What are two ways that the rat kangaroo and the kangaroo rat are alike?

_____

6. What are some differences between the two animals?

_____

Read the passage. Complete the graphic organizer. Then answer the questions.

Dolphins are mammals. Marine dolphins live in saltwater. Although they can be found in most of the world's oceans, some dolphins don't live in the ocean. River dolphins live in freshwater rivers in South America and Asia. The adults are about five to eight feet long. On the other hand, marine dolphins can be 30 feet long. There are about 40 types of marine dolphins, but only seven types of river dolphins. Marine dolphins see well, but river dolphins have very small eyes. They are almost blind. Like marine dolphins, river dolphins eat fish, but they have a different method for finding food. They find their food by using their snouts to root through the mud at the bottom of the river.

	Marine Dolphins	River Dolphins
Fish or Mammal?		
Home		
Size		
Number of Types		
Food		
Sight		

1. What signal words does the writer use in the passage to compare and contrast?

_____

_____

2. Based on the chart, write two sentences telling how marine dolphins and river dolphins are alike and how they are different.

_____

_____

Read the passage. Then circle the letter of the answer to each question.

The kiwi is a rare and strange bird. Unlike most birds, the kiwi has a keen sense of smell. Most birds have nostrils at the base of their beaks, but the kiwi's nostrils are at the end of its bill. Unlike most other birds, kiwis emit a strong smell when they preen their feathers. Researchers say kiwis smell like mushrooms or ammonia. Another unusual thing about the kiwi is its brown feathers. They look and feel like hair. The kiwi also has hairs near its bill that look like whiskers. Like a cat, a kiwi uses the whiskers to find its way in the dark. The strangest thing is that the kiwi does not fly. It runs fast.

1. What is the main thing to which the writer compares and contrasts the kiwi?

   A hair

   B fruit

   C cats

   D other birds

2. To what is the smell of the kiwi compared?

   F a cat

   G mushrooms

   H feathers

   J hair

3. The kiwi's feathers are different from those of other birds because

   A they are brown.

   B they are like hair.

   C they are soft.

   D they are near its bill.

4. One difference between kiwis and other birds is

   F how they smell.

   G what they eat.

   H how they see.

   J how they sound.

5. What can you learn about most other birds from the passage?

   A They have whiskers.

   B They are like cats.

   C They have brown feathers.

   D They do not emit a strong smell.

6. In what way is a kiwi similar to a cat?

   F They both smell like ammonia.

   G They both have soft feathers.

   H They both use whiskers to find their way in the dark.

   J They both emit a strong smell when they groom themselves.

Workplace Skill:
Compare and Contrast Information in a Table

Tables help you to compare and contrast information. They put ideas and data side by side so that you can classify, or arrange, important ideas or numbers.

The table below provides information about "green" jobs. A green job contributes to preserving the quality of the environment. The processing of renewable energy sources creates many of today's green jobs.

Read the information in the table. Then circle the letter of the answer to each question.

Estimated Employment in the Renewable Energy Sector, Selected Countries, 2006

Renewable Energy Source	World Employment*	Selected Countries	National Employment
Wind	at least 207,100	Germany	82,100
		United States	36,800
		Spain	35,000
		China	22,200
		Denmark	21,000
		India	10,000
Solar thermal	at least 624,342	China	600,000
		Germany	13,300
		Spain	9,142
		United States	1,900
Hydropower	at least 39,000	Europe	20,000
		United States	19,000
Geothermal	at least 25,200	United States	21,000
		Germany	4,200

*Countries for which information is available.
Source: Green Jobs UNEP/ILO/IOE/ITUC, September 2008

1. In Germany, how does the number of people working in wind power compare to those working in geothermal power?

   A There are fewer people working in geothermal power.

   B There are more people working in geothermal power.

   C The numbers are the same.

   D There are no people working in either field.

2. If you wanted a job in the renewable energy sector in the United States, which area offers the highest potential for employment?

   F wind

   G solar thermal

   H hydropower

   J geothermal

Write for Work

You work for a global environmental agency. Using the table on page 146, you are preparing a report on employment in the renewable energy field. Use clue words to describe the situation of employment in the renewable energy sector in 2006. Which countries were leading in what areas? Which countries were lagging behind? Write your report in a notebook.

 Reading Extension

Turn to "Together Again after 50 Years" on page 89 of *Reading Basics Introductory Reader*. After you have read and/or listened to the article, answer the questions below.

Circle the letter of the answer to each question.

1. How were the actions of North and South Korean officials in 1950 different compared to their actions in 2000?

   A In 1950 they allowed people to contact their families, but in 2000 they did not.

   B In 1950 the officials only allowed families to call one another, but in 2000 they allowed visits.

   C In 1950 the officials did not allow any contact between family members, but in 2000 they allowed supervised visits.

   D In 1950 the officials allowed letters between families, but in 2000 they only allowed e-mails.

2. What is one difference between Ryang's siblings and his mother during the visit?

   F His siblings were angry at Ryang, but his mother was happy to see him.

   G His siblings were happy to see him, but his mother was angry.

   H His siblings were able to make it to the hotel, but his mother could not.

   J His mother was able to make it to the hotel, but his siblings could not.

3. What is one thing that Ryang and his mother had in common during their separation?

   A They each remembered and thought of one another.

   B They both worked for the government.

   C They were both very sick.

   D They could write and call each other.

Write the answer to each question.

4. What is one thing that many people in North and South Korea had in common?

   _____

5. How does the author compare Ryang's feelings with those of the general public?

   _____

Explore Words

LONG *i* AND LONG *o*

The letter *i* alone can stand for the long *i* sound, as in the word *kind*. The letter *o* alone can stand for the long *o* sound, as in the word *colt*.

Read the sentences. Circle the word with a long vowel sound to complete each sentence.

1. (Most, Some) of my friends have good jobs.
2. Mr. Garcia (got, sold) his car online.
3. What class is your (child, kid) in?

4. Have you (told, asked) the teacher about that?
5. Can you help me (fix, find) my glasses?
6. I plan to (host, give) a party in June.

SPELLING: PLURALS

Plural nouns are nouns that name more than one thing. To make most nouns plural, add -*s* to the end of the word (*student/students*). To form the plural of words that end with *s*, *ss*, *sh*, *x*, or *ch*, add -*es* (*boss/bosses*). For words that end in *y*, change the *y* to *i* and add -*es* (*penny/pennies*). For most words that end with *f* or *ff*, add -*s* to form the plural (*chiefs*, *spoofs*, *staffs*). For some words that end with *f*, change the final *f* to -*ves*. (*half/halves*). For words that end in -*fe*, first change the *f* to *v*, and then add -*s* (*wife/wives*). Use a dictionary if you are not sure.

Write the plural form of each word on the line.

1. fax _____

2. baby _____

3. leaf _____

4. boss _____

5. peach _____

6. wish _____

7. chef _____

8. life _____

SPELLING: HOMOPHONES

Homophones are words that sound alike but do not look the same or mean the same thing. For example, the words *son* and *sun* are homophones. The word *son* means "a male child." The sun is the center of our solar system.

Circle the homophone that correctly completes each sentence.

1. Marvin caught a fish from the (see, sea).
2. The dinner plate held one (roli, role).
3. Leila wore the belt on her (waste, waist).
4. I want (to, two) stop smoking.
5. He (wood, would) buy a car if he had enough money.

Two vowels that come together usually stand for the long vowel sound of the first letter. Read these examples:

Vowel Sound	Vowel Pair	Examples
Long *a*	*ai, ay*	train, spray
Long *e*	*ea, ee*	speak, green
Long *i*	*ie*	tie, pie
Long *o*	*oa, oe*	soap, toe
Long *u*	*ue*	fuel, true

Choose a vowel pair to complete each word. Write the vowel pair on the line.

1. The cafeteria is serving pork r_____st today. (ai, oa)

2. When are these library books d_____? (ue, ie)

3. Let's set up a pl_____ date for the kids. (ee, ay)

4. I didn't get very much sl_____p last night. (oe, ee)

5. He bought a new t_____. (ai, ie)

6. A female deer is called a d_____. (oe, ay)

7. The water goes down the dr_____n. (ai, ea)

8. We took in a str_____ cat last week. (ie, ay)

9. The waves at the b_____ch were huge! (ue, ea)

10. Her bike is bl_____. (ue, ie)

Knowing these high-frequency words will help you in many school subjects.

compare	to show how things are alike
contrast	to show how things are different
respond	to react to something
method	a particular way of doing something
rare	not occurring very often

Complete the sentences below using one of the words above.

1. Elizabeth did not _____ well to the new medicine.

2. The museum has many _____ coins on display.

3. When you _____ two things, you mention similarities.

4. Rylee's _____ for keeping her house clean was unusual but effective.

5. Dante listed differences between bikes and cars in order to _____ them.

Lesson 3.3

Identify Author's Purpose

Authors typically write for one or more of the following purposes: to persuade, to inform, to explain, to entertain, or to describe. Sometimes, an author has more than one purpose. Identifying the author's purpose or purposes will help you better understand what you read.

To identify the author's purpose, ask yourself questions. For example, have I been informed of anything by reading the passage? Are the people and events in the passage real or made up? The author's purpose in a passage about made-up people might be to entertain rather than to inform.

Read the following example. The author's purpose is to explain the step-by-step process of making butter.

> Butter is made from the fat in cream. When cream is shaken, the fat comes together. It forms bits of butter. After the butter bits have formed, a liquid is left. This liquid is called buttermilk. The buttermilk is drained off. Next, the butter bits are washed with cold water. Then they are drained and salted. In the final stage, the butter is mixed well.

This passage gives readers information about how butter is made. You can infer from the explanations that the author's purpose was to explain how to make butter. When you know the author's purpose is to teach you something, you may pay better attention to stated concepts and details. If you know that the author's purpose is to tell an entertaining story, you may read in a more relaxed way.

Read the passage. What is the author's purpose?

> Gilberto Costa was a smoker. He started smoking when he was 17 years old. Now Gil was 40 years old. He was smoking two packs of cigarettes a day. Gil knew that he could not breathe as well as he used to. He got tired when he climbed stairs and when he played with his kids. He would cough a lot and have to rest. His doctor was worried. She told Gil that cigarettes are the leading cause of lung cancer. She told him to stop smoking.

This passage warns readers about the dangers of smoking cigarettes and gives information about how smoking affects the body. The author's purpose is to keep readers from starting to smoke. If they already smoke, the author would like to persuade them to stop.

Read each passage. Circle the letter of the answer to each question.

> Rico wanted to see the free opera, but he was afraid his friends would laugh at him. Rico went into the hall quietly, after making sure no one he knew was nearby. When the curtain rose, music filled the hall. For the next several hours, Rico listened to the musicians perform as the story unfolded. At the end, he clapped for an encore.

1. What is the author's purpose for writing this passage?

   A   to persuade readers to go to an opera

   B   to entertain with a story

   C   to explain how operas unfold

   D   to describe the concert hall

> Jet lag is a condition that people get when they travel to another time zone. It happens because people have an internal clock. Our internal clocks help run our bodies. Say you leave New York at 7:00 P.M. and land in London six hours later. Your body thinks that it is 1:00 A.M. and wants to sleep. However, it is 7:00 A.M. in London—time to start the day! Jet lag will make you feel sleepy during the day and unable to sleep at night. Your internal clock will reset itself at some point, but it may take several days. Then you will have to adjust again when you fly home.

2. What is the author's purpose for writing this passage?

   F   to persuade readers to get more sleep

   G   to amuse or entertain readers

   H   to persuade readers not to travel

   J   to explain jet lag

> If chewing gum gets into a carpet, it can be a big problem. However, there is an easy method for removing it. Freeze the gum with an ice cube. The ice will cause the gum to harden. When the gum gets hard enough, scrape it out of the carpet with a table knife.

3. What is the author's purpose for writing this passage?

   A   to describe what chewing gum tastes like

   B   to inform readers about the history of chewing gum

   C   to persuade readers not to chew gum

   D   to explain how to remove chewing gum from a carpet

Read each passage. Then answer the questions.

If you burn your skin, you can speed up the healing process with good first aid. Here is what you should do. First, evaluate the burn. Does it look white or black instead of red? Does it feel numb? Is it larger than a three-inch square? If the answer to any of these questions is yes, seek medical help. If the answers are no, it is probably a minor burn. Run cool (NOT cold) water over the burn to stop the burning process. The water will also lessen the pain. DO NOT apply aloe vera, butter, or any ointment to the burn—doing so could cause infection.

1. What is the author's purpose?

_____

2. What clues in the passage helped you understand the purpose?

_____

3. Do you think the author achieved his or her purpose? Why or why not?

_____

On the edge of a small village, big waves crash into jagged, tall cliffs. From the cliffs, green grass stretches inland as far as the eye can see. The air smells like seawater. Cows and sheep dot the rolling landscape. A stone church seems to bathe in sunlight atop an empty hill. Down the main road, inns, pubs, a music shop, and a bicycle shop line the street. From the cliff, everything is peaceful. The only sound is the roar of the waves. On the main road, cars and people pass by.

4. What is the author's purpose?

_____

5. What clues in the passage helped you understand the purpose?

_____

_____

6. Do you think the author achieves his or her purpose? Why or why not?

_____

Read each passage. Then circle the letter of the answer to each question.

Many people would guess that Greenland got its name because the land is so green, but they would be wrong. Greenland is not green. It is even icier than Iceland. Greenland was named to confuse people. In A.D. 982 a Norse explorer discovered this island. It was bitter cold there, and the land was covered with ice and snow. The explorer wanted people to move there to start a colony, so he named it Greenland. The trick worked! Soon 25 ships full of settlers sailed for the icy land.

1. What is the author's main purpose for writing this passage?

   A to amuse readers with a made-up story

   B to explain the origin of a name

   C to describe Norse life long ago

   D to teach readers about sites in Greenland

Eight out of 10 drivers say they use their cell phones while driving. It is tempting to use your cell phone while you drive, but don't do it! Both texting and talking cause drivers to be inattentive. Being distracted is the leading cause of car accidents. In 2008 about 6,000 people were killed and about a half million people were injured in crashes because drivers were not paying attention. It is likely that many of the drivers in those crashes were using cell phones.

2. What is the author's main purpose for writing this passage?

   F to amuse readers with a story

   G to describe the best driving practices

   H to persuade people to not use cell phones while driving

   J to teach readers how to drive

In Sweden, there is a hotel made of ice. The walls, floors, and all the furniture are built each year from ice and snow. Visitors wear long underwear and woolen hats. They sleep in thermal sleeping bags on top of ice beds.

3. What is the author's main purpose for writing this passage?

   A to describe the ice hotel

   B to explain how the ice hotel is built

   C to persuade readers to visit the ice hotel

   D to teach readers about the properties of ice

Workplace Skill:
Identify Author's Purpose in a Memo

Memos are brief written messages used in companies. Memos are usually e-mails. They help employees communicate with each other. Company memos can be written for several purposes, including to inform employees of events. The memo below is an invitation to a "Webinar," or a workshop over the web.

Read the memo. Then circle the letter of the answer to each question below the box.

From: Corporate Communications and Human Resources
Sent: Thursday, September 16
To: All Employees
Subject: First-Aid Webinar

Did you know that the Heimlich maneuver has changed? Are you up to date on the latest emergency-preparedness issues for you and your family? Join Corporate Communications and Human Resources for a Webinar to learn the latest issues in first aid.

Corporate Communications and Human Resources will present an interactive session on first aid for home and work. The latest tips on first aid and safety will be covered.

Join us for this informative session.

First Aid at Work and at Home
Friday, September 24, Lakeshore Conference Room
12:30 P.M. – Lunch
1:00 P.M. – Webinar

Space is limited. Register today by sending an e-mail to Corporate Communications. Webinar details will be provided after you register.

---

1. What is the author's purpose for writing this memo?

   A   to outline the company's first-aid policy

   B   to invite employees to a presentation

   C   to explain how a Webinar works

   D   to tell employees about the Corporate Communications department

2. If you want to participate in the Webinar, what do you need to do?

   F   register by e-mail

   G   be present for the lunch at 12:30 P.M.

   H   contact a Webinar representative

   J   contact Human Resources

Write for Work

Your manager has asked you to send a memo by e-mail to your fellow employees. You are supposed to invite them to an upcoming company meeting. Think about your purpose for writing. Think about the details you need to include in the memo. What do your fellow employees need to know? Think about what you should include in a good memo. Write the memo in a notebook.

  Reading Extension

Turn to "A Special Kind of Horse Power" on page 97 of *Reading Basics Introductory Reader*. After you have read and/or listened to the article, answer the questions below.

Circle the letter of the answer to each question.

1. What is the author's purpose for writing this selection?

   A to describe types of special needs that children have

   B to persuade horse owners to make their horses available to special-needs children

   C to explain how horseback riding can help some children with special needs

   D to help parents identify the needs of their children

2. Who do you think might benefit most from reading this article?

   F parents and teachers of special-needs children

   G children who have asthma

   H people who like to ride horses

   J horseback-riding instructors

3. Why is it good for special-needs children to ride horses?

   A Most horses are not gentle.

   B Horses walk in the same way humans do.

   C Horses do not accept children unless they are performing perfectly.

   D Horses are slow to bond with riders.

Write the answer to each question.

4. Describe two ways that riding horses can help children with special needs.

   _____

5. What is one helpful thing that you could do with the information in the article?

   _____

Explore Words

VOWEL COMBINATIONS

Some vowel combinations stand for the long vowel sound of the first letter in the pair. The vowel pairs *oi* and *oy* stand for a different sound. They stand for the sound you hear in the middle of *soil* and at the end of *enjoy*. Vowel pair *oi* is usually seen in the middle of a word. Vowel pair *oy* is usually seen at the end of a syllable or word.

point	destroy	poisonous	voyage
spoiled	noise	choice	annoy

Choose a word from the box to complete each sentence. Write the word on the line.

1. It is not polite to _____ at people.

2. We have the _____ between chili and vegetable soup.

3. A cobra is a _____ snake.

4. Did the hurricane _____ any homes?

5. My mother thinks that my kids are _____.

6. Good-bye! I hope you have a wonderful _____!

7. The baby is napping, so don't make a lot of _____.

8. Sales calls during dinner usually _____ people.

SYLLABLES

Many words end in a consonant + *le*. In words such as *table, sample,* and *middle,* the consonant + *le* always stay in the same syllable: ta / ble, sam / ple, mid / dle. To read consonant + *le* words, determine whether the first syllable is open or closed. If it is open, the vowel sound is long. If it is closed, the vowel sound is short.

Look at the syllables. If the first syllable is open, write *long*. If the first syllable is closed, write *short*.

1. ti / tle _____

2. han / dle _____

3. mid / dle _____

4. stee / ple _____

5. gen / tle _____

6. nee / dle _____

PREFIXES *pre-*, *in-*

A prefix is a word part that can be added to the beginning of a word. Adding a prefix to a word changes the meaning of the word. *Pre-* and *in-* are prefixes. *Pre-* means "before," and *in-* can mean "not."

pre + heat	Please **preheat** the oven and then put in the cookies. *Preheat* means "heat before."
in + tolerant	My school principal is **intolerant** of bullies. *Intolerant* means "not tolerant."

For each word, form a new word by adding the prefix *pre-* or *in-*. Then write the new word and its meaning.

1. dawn _____

2. complete _____

3. judge _____

4. visible _____

5. frequent _____

6. sane _____

ACADEMIC VOCABULARY

Knowing these high-frequency words will help you in many school subjects.

events   things that happen

intention   a goal or plan

explain   to give enough details to make the meaning clear

minor   slight or unimportant

persuade   to convince someone to do something

Complete the sentences below using one of the words above.

1. They found a _____ problem and solved it right away.

2. The book covered all the important _____ in his life.

3. I have no _____ of spoiling the surprise.

4. You will need to _____ your symptoms to the doctor.

5. Peer pressure can _____ teens to do dangerous things.

Lesson 3.4

Use Graphs

Graphs give information visually. The most common graphs are circle graphs, line graphs, and bar graphs. Bar graphs and line graphs organize information using axes. A vertical axis is a line that goes up and down. A horizontal axis usually goes along the bottom. Bar graphs compare groups of data. Information is shown on a set of bars. Line graphs show change over time. On a line graph, the changing data is shown on a continuous line. A circle graph does not have axes. It is divided into pieces, like a pie. Each piece represents a different part of the whole. When the parts of a circle graph are expressed in a percentage, the parts add up to 100 percent.

Graphs usually illustrate text information. When reading a graph, first study the title and the labels on the axes. The labels tell the scale. Read this graph:

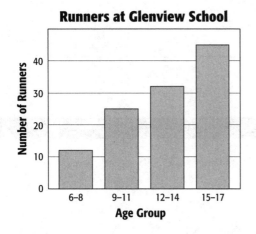

The title tells what the graph is about. The vertical axis shows the number of runners. Each horizontal line represents 10 runners. The bars represent the age groups. If the top of a bar falls between two horizontal lines, estimate the value.

Read the graph. Then answer the questions.

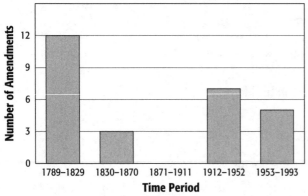

How many amendments does each line on the vertical axis represent? Contrast this graph and the first graph.

Each line represents three amendments. In the first graph, each line represents 10 runners. In this graph, the bars represent time periods. In the first graph, they represent age groups.

Use the line graph to answer the questions.

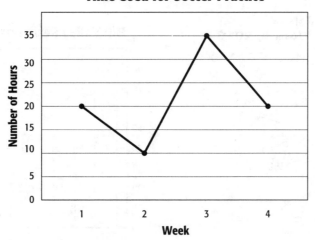

Time Used for Soccer Practice

1. During which week did the team practice the most hours?

   _____

2. What was the least number of hours practiced in one week?

   _____

3. How many fewer hours did the team practice in Week 4 than in Week 3?

   _____

4. What is the difference between the greatest and the least number of hours practiced?

   _____

5. During which weeks did the team practice the same number of hours?

   _____

6. In which week did the number of hours of practice drop by 15 from the week before?

   _____

7. In which week did the number of hours of practice increase by 25 from the week before?

   _____

8. In which week did the number of hours of practice drop by 10 from the week before?

   _____

Use the graphs to answer the questions.

Graph A

**How Hill Valley
Residents Got to Work in 2010**

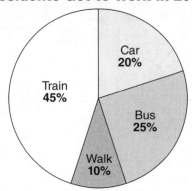

Graph B

Hill Valley Residents Who Walk to Work

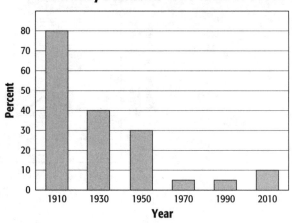

1. What percent of Hill Valley residents got to work by bus in 2010? _____

2. What method of transportation did the most residents of Hill Valley use to get to work in 2010?

   _____

3. Which statement about Hill Valley residents in 2010 is true? Circle the letter of the answer.

   A There were fewer train riders than bus riders.

   B Train riders made up more than one-half of the commuters.

   C There were more walkers than bus riders.

   D There were as many train riders as there were bus riders and car riders together.

4. Which graph shows changes in the percentage of people who walk to work? _____

5. Which of the following is a true statement about Hill Valley residents? Circle your answer.

   F The percentage of walkers has steadily increased.

   G 1950 had the least percentage of people who walk to work.

   H The percentage of walkers is less in 2010 than in 1910.

   J The percentage of walkers has stayed the same from 1910 to 2010.

6. What other type of graph could you use to show the change in Hill Valley residents who walked to work over the past 100 years?

   _____

Use the graphs to answer the questions.

Graph A

**Favorite Composers of Audiences
for Royal Orchestra Tour**

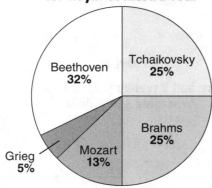

Graph B

**Average Size of Audiences for
Royal Orchestra Tour**

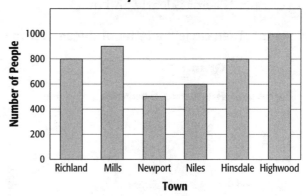

1. Which towns had the same average size audiences for the Royal Orchestra Tour?

   A Niles, Hinsdale

   B Newport, Niles

   C Richland, Hinsdale

   D Newport, Richland

2. What was the average size audience for Newport?

   F about 700

   G 600

   H about 500

   J 400

3. Which composer was the favorite of the fewest people?

   A Grieg

   B Mozart

   C Brahms

   D Beethoven

4. Which composer was the audiences' favorite?

   F Brahms

   G Beethoven

   H Tchaikovsky

   J Grieg

5. What percentage of the audiences preferred Tchaikovsky?

   A 32%

   B 25%

   C 13%

   D 5%

6. What was the average size of audiences for Highwood?

   F 800 people

   G 900 people

   H 1000 people

   J 1100 people

7. Which town had the smallest audience?

   A Mills

   B Newport

   C Niles

   D Hinsdale

8. What percentage of the audiences preferred Mozart?

   F 32%

   G 25%

   H 13%

   J 5%

Workplace Skill: Use Graphs in a Business Environment

Graphs are used in business environments to show data. Graphs are an easy way to look at and make sense of data. With graphs, you can easily explain your information and get your point across clearly and quickly.

Read the graph. Then circle the letter of the answer to each question.

Graph A

Baseball Revenue Sources

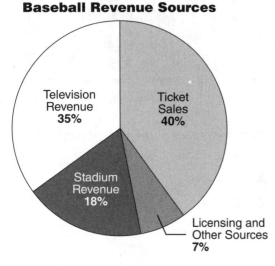

Graph B

Baseball Revenue from a Team Averaging $66 Million

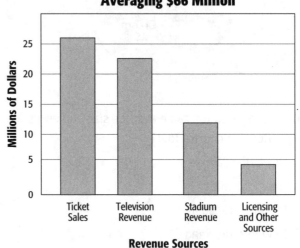

1. You are a financial manager for a baseball team. If you wanted to find the percentage of revenue from ticket sales, which graph would you use?

   A   Graph B

   B   Graphs A and B

   C   Graph A

   D   neither Graph A nor Graph B

2. Which revenue source yields about 22 million dollars?

   F   ticket sales

   G   stadium revenue

   H   licensing and other sources

   J   television revenue

3. What percentage of baseball revenue sources comes from ticket sales?

   A   40%

   B   7%

   C   18%

   D   35%

4. What is the smallest source of baseball revenue?

   F   ticket sales

   G   stadium revenue

   H   licensing and other sources

   J   television revenue

Write for Work

As a financial manager for a baseball team, you need to prepare a report about the team's revenue sources. Use Graphs A and B from page 162. Prepare the report in paragraph form. Detail the percentages and dollar amounts for each of the four revenue sources listed.

 Reading Extension

Turn to "Racing through the Pain" on page 105 of *Reading Basics Introductory Reader*. After you have read and/or listened to the article, answer the questions below.

Circle the letter of the answer to each question.

1. What is one nickname by which Kristin Strode-Penny is known?

    A Speed Racer

    B Xena, the Warrior Princess

    C Kristina, the Kiwi

    D Parasite Penny

2. Why did Strode-Penny take up adventure racing?

    F She needed the prize money to pay off debts.

    G She needed a hobby.

    H She wanted to travel and see the world.

    J Adventure racing combined the skills she already had.

3. Which was the first task with which Seagate struggled?

    A cutting down trees and vines

    B scrambling up waterfalls

    C trudging through mud

    D building a raft from bamboo poles

4. What does Seagate say was the reason for their victory?

    F They were better rested than the other teams.

    G All of the other teams dropped out of the race.

    H None of the team members struggled with foot troubles.

    J They practiced more than the other teams.

Write the answer to the question.

5. What happened to Strode-Penny after the race?

_____

Explore Words

VOWEL COMBINATIONS

Some vowel combinations stand for the long vowel sound of the first letter in the pair. However, some vowel combinations can stand for a different sound. The vowel combinations *au* and *aw* stand for the sound you hear in the middle of *pause* and at the end of *jaw*. The letters *ow* and *ou* sometimes stand for the sound you hear at the end of *cow* and in the middle of *house*.

sauce	awful	spouse	allow

Choose a word from the box to complete each sentence. Write the word on the line.

1. A _____ is a husband or wife.

2. The storm has made an _____ mess of the yard.

3. I do not _____ my kids to watch TV after school.

4. Elliot's tomato _____ has a lot of spice in it.

SYLLABLES

Many words have one consonant appearing between two vowels, such as *robin*. When deciding how to divide words such as these into syllables, first try dividing the word before the consonant (ro / bin). The first syllable is open and has a long vowel sound. If the word doesn't sound right, divide the word after the consonant: (rob / in). Now the first syllable is closed, and the pronunciation is correct.

Each word is broken into syllables in two different ways. Circle the letter that shows how the word should be divided so that it sounds right.

1. tiger
   a. ti / ger
   b. tig / er

2. wagon
   a. wa / gon
   b. wag / on

3. pilot
   a. pi / lot
   b. pil / ot

4. cabin
   a. ca / bin
   b. cab / in

5. habit
   a. ha / bit
   b. hab / it

6. music
   a. mu / sic
   b. mus / ic

SPELLING: SUFFIXES *-able, -er*

A suffix is a word part that can be added to the end of a word. The suffix *-able* means "able to," and the suffix *-er* means "someone who." For example, the word *fixable* means "able to be fixed," and *teacher* means "someone who teaches." When adding the suffixes *-able* and *-er*, spelling rules may apply:

- If a word ends in silent *e*, you usually drop the *e*. Then add the suffix.

    size + able = sizable   *write + er = writer*

- If a word ends in a single vowel followed by a single consonant, you usually double the consonant. Then add the suffix.

    regret + able = regrettable   *jog + er = jogger*

- If a word ends in a consonant and *y*, change the *y* to *i* and add the suffix.

    deny + able = deniable   *copy + er = copier*

Add the suffix to the word. Write the new word on the line.

1. paint + er _____

2. adapt + able _____

3. adore + able _____

4. win + er _____

5. break + able _____

6. garden + er _____

7. supply + er _____

8. drum + er _____

ACADEMIC VOCABULARY

Knowing these high-frequency words will help you in many school subjects.

graph a visual way to show data

data facts and statistics collected together

illustrate to explain or make clear

label word or words that tell what things represent

estimate to roughly calculate the value of something

Complete the sentences below using one of the words above.

1. The _____ from the experiment were not what the researcher had hoped for.

2. To get ready for his camping trip, Tito will _____ how much food he'll need.

3. Kalila put a _____ on each container of leftovers in the fridge.

4. The instructions included a diagram to _____ how to assemble the desk.

5. The _____ showed that the temperature had gone up each day last week.

Lesson 3.5

Read Signs

People used symbols and pictures to communicate long before there was a written language. In math, symbols tell you when to add, subtract, multiply, or divide. On maps, symbols identify cities, roads, and other landmarks. There are symbols on the labels in your clothes to tell you how to wash them.

You may see symbols on signs. Some signs have words, but others have only symbols. Each symbol has a meaning that helps you understand a concept. You will see signs on roads and public buildings. It is important to understand what these signs mean.

Look at the following signs:

The sign on the left is a picture of a person about to board a bus. This sign means "bus stop." The sign in the middle has a large X and two Rs. This sign means "railroad crossing." The two Rs stand for "railroad," and the X looks like two roads crossing. The sign on the right shows two people crossing the street. This sign means "pedestrian crossing." One of the most common symbols, shown below, is a backward slash that means "no" or "don't."

Look at the signs below and figure out what they mean.

The sign on the left shows a truck with the symbol for *no* over it. It means that trucks are not allowed. The sign on the right has a picture of a tent, which stands for a campground.

Reading Basics · Introductory

Signs give many kinds of information, including warnings about dangerous products or situations.

Look at each warning sign. What does it mean? Choose the meaning from the list. Then write the meaning on the line.

signal ahead	divided highway	bicycle route
no smoking	deer crossing	fire hazard
steep hill	children playing	slippery when wet
merge		

1.  _____

2.  _____

3.  _____

4. _____

5.  _____

6.  _____

7.  _____

8.  _____

9.  _____

10.  _____

Look at each sign. Then write the letter of each answer on the lines.

1. Which sign tells you that you are not allowed to make a U-turn? _____

2. Which sign tells you that a parking space is reserved for people with disabilities? _____

3. Which sign tells you that right turns are not allowed? _____

4. Which sign tells you about a campsite where tents can be used? _____

5. Which sign tells you there is a gas station ahead? _____

6. Which sign tells you not to enter? _____

7. Which sign tells what highway you are on? _____

8. Which sign tells you that passing is not allowed? _____

9. Which sign tells you that a steep downhill grade is ahead? _____

Circle the letter of the answer that gives the meaning of each sign.

1.

   A   railroad crossing

   B   telephone

   C   pedestrian crossing

   D   no passing zone

2.

   F   hospital

   G   campground

   H   crosswalk

   J   no left turn

3.

   A   no right turn

   B   no U-turn

   C   no trucks

   D   recycle

4.

   F   bus stop

   G   biohazard

   H   airport

   J   do not enter

5.

   A   listen

   B   stop

   C   look

   D   slow

6.

   F   pedestrian crossing

   G   deer crossing

   H   railroad crossing

   J   bus stop

7.

   A   pedestrian crossing

   B   children playing

   C   camping

   D   bus stop

8.

   F   fire hazard

   G   no passing zone

   H   camping

   J   hospital

9.

   A   bus stop

   B   don't walk

   C   no crossing

   D   hospital

10.

   F   no trucks

   G   warning

   H   no right turn

   J   no smoking

Workplace Skill:
Use Signs in the Workplace

Signs are used in the workplace to communicate information. Signs can help you navigate through the space where you work, whether it be in a factory, a restaurant, or an office. Signs can provide safety information. They can also include specific directions to serve certain employee needs.

Look at each sign. Then write the letter of each answer on the lines.

1. Which sign would be very important for a food service worker to follow? _____

2. Which sign warns of a risk of fire? _____

3. Which sign tells you whether or not you can smoke? _____

4. Which sign might be at the entrance to a meeting room? _____

5. Which sign means a wheelchair can move easily in the building? _____

6. Which sign shows the location of a stairway? _____

7. Which sign might stop someone from collecting donations? _____

8. Which sign would be posted where quiet is needed? _____

Write for Work

Your manager wants you to make a list of workplace signs. You need to think of all the possible signs your place of work will need before it opens to the public. What signs are needed to give information about where things are? What signs are needed to ensure the safety of your coworkers? Write your list in a notebook.

 Reading Extension

Turn to "In the Face of Danger" on page 113 of *Reading Basics Introductory Reader*. After you have read and/or listened to the article, answer the questions below.

Circle the letter of the answer to each question.

1. Why did protestors think McKeel was with the KKK?

    A   He had been up on stage at the rally.

    B   He had an image of the Confederate flag on his shirt.

    C   He was yelling at the protestors.

    D   He closely resembled the leader of the Klan at the rally.

2. What did Keshia Thomas's principal think of her actions?

    F   He felt she should not have put herself in danger.

    G   He felt she was too young to be at the rally.

    H   He thought she should have stopped the attackers with words.

    J   He thought her actions were noble.

3. Why did Thomas risk herself to save McKeel?

    A   She wanted to end the cycle of violence.

    B   She thought he wasn't a member of the KKK.

    C   She thought the police should arrest him.

    D   She wanted a chance to yell at him.

Write the answer to each question.

4. Based on the article, what can you conclude about how Thomas felt about the attention she received?

_____

5. Do you think Thomas did the right thing by saving McKeel? Explain why or why not.

_____

_____

Explore Words

Vowel combinations such as *aw* and *oi* stand for only one sound. Other vowel combinations have more than one possible sound. The vowel pair *oo* has two different sounds. It stands for the long *u* sound that you hear in the middle of *food*. It also stands for the sound that you hear in the middle of *book*.

Choose the vowel combination that completes each word. Write it on the line.

1. Please l_____k at me when I'm talking to you. (oo, aw)

2. Clarita woke up at d_____n. (aw, ow)

3. Are you going to fry that meat or br_____l it? (oi, oo)

4. The dentist might have to pull that t_____th. (aw, oo)

BASE WORDS

A base word is a word that does not include any prefix, suffix, or other word part. Look at the word *misspelled*. The prefix *mis-* and the ending *-ed* were added to the base word *spell*.

Write the base word in each of the following words on the line.

1. sorrowful _____

2. previewing _____

3. incorrect _____

4. cloudless _____

5. revisited _____

6. dreamer _____

SPELLING: POSSESSIVES

An apostrophe (') is used to write possessive words. Words that end in *'s* show that something belongs to one person or thing. Words that end in *s'* show that something belongs to more than one person or thing. The words *my cousins' house* show that the house belongs to two or more cousins.

Read each phrase. Use *'s* or *s'* to write the possessive phrase on the line.

1. the garden of my grandmother _____

2. the hotel of the travelers _____

3. the route of the explorer _____

4. the paintings of the artists _____

When you add suffixes or other endings to words, remember these spelling rules:

- If a word ends in silent *e* and the suffix or other word ending begins with a vowel, you usually drop the *e*. Then you add the word ending.

    scrape + -ed = scraped   *lame + -est = lamest*

- If a word ends in a vowel followed by a consonant and the word ending begins with a vowel, you usually double the consonant. Then add the word ending.

    regret + -able = regrettable   *drop + -ing = dropping*

- If a word ends in a consonant and *y*, you usually change the *y* to *i*. Then you add the word ending.

    duty + -ful = dutiful   *copy + -er = copier*

Read each word. If the word is misspelled, spell it correctly. If it is correct, write *correct*.

1. floodes _____

2. predictable _____

3. erasing _____

4. hopless _____

5. valueable _____

6. helpful _____

7. rainless _____

8. bankes _____

9. washed _____

10. carryed _____

ACADEMIC VOCABULARY

Knowing these high-frequency words will help you in many school subjects.

communicate	to tell by speaking, writing, or gesturing
concrete	specific or definite
abstract	indicating an idea, quality, or state
correspond	to have a close similarity
examine	to inspect or study closely

Complete the sentences below using one of the words above.

1. The judge did not want to hear opinions. She wanted _____ details.

2. Nizhoni wanted to _____ the cell under a microscope.

3. The marks on the wall did not _____ to the children's heights anymore.

4. _____ poetry can be difficult to understand because of its complicated ideas.

5. It was easier to _____ my ideas over the phone than in an e-mail.

Lesson 3.6

Use a Dictionary

A dictionary defines a word. It also gives the pronunciation, the part of speech, and the history of the word. You can use a dictionary to look up the definition, or meaning, of a word you don't know. Most words have more than one definition. You can also check the spelling of a word in a dictionary.

Dictionary words are arranged in alphabetical order. To list words in alphabetical order, look at the first letter in each word. List the words in the order of the alphabet.

> bet
> dollar
> grant

If the first letters are the same, look at the second letter. If the second letters are the same, look at the third, and so on.

> danger
> dream
> drip

Two guide words appear at the top of each dictionary page. The guide word on the left is the same as the first entry word on the page. The guide word on the right is the same as the last entry word on the page. The other words on the page are listed in alphabetical order between the guide words.

If the guide words at the top of a dictionary page are *gong* and *gourd*, for example, then words such as *good* and *goose* also appear on the page. They come in alphabetical order between *gong* and *gourd*. Guide words help you find words more quickly. If you were looking for *gopher*, you would know that it is on the page between *gong* and *gourd*. The word *gopher* comes in alphabetical order between those two words.

Match each word on the left to the correct pair of dictionary guide words on the right.

lapse	cell • cement
control	constant • converge
cello	lap • lard

You should have matched *lapse* with *lap* and *lard*. *Cello* is in between *cell* and *cement*. *Control* is in between *constant* and *converge*. The entry words come in alphabetical order between the guide words with which they are matched.

A dictionary shows how to pronounce words. These written pronunciations use letters and symbols to represent sounds. Consonants stand for consonant sounds. Vowels without symbols above them represent short vowel sounds. Vowels with symbols above them stand for other vowel sounds. Ask your teacher to read the following words aloud so you can match the sounds with the symbols.

rake (rāk)   her (hər)   tree (trē)   good (gu̇d)
write (rīt)   food (füd)   boat (bōt)   ball (bȯl)

Use a dictionary to look up the pronunciations for these words. Write the pronunciations you find in the dictionary.

1. boot _____

2. heard _____

3. strike _____

4. crawl _____

5. clean _____

6. time _____

7. toad _____

8. brake _____

9. green _____

10. hall _____

Ask your teacher to read the words in the box aloud. Match each word with its pronunciation and write the word on the line. The symbol (') means a spoken stress.

bail	dime	call	laugh	fall
invade	cashier	road	seen	jewel
bake	giraffe	brook	better	haze

11. (ˈkȯl) _____

12. (ka ˈshir) _____

13. (bru̇k) _____

14. (in ˈvād) _____

15. (hāz) _____

16. (bāl) _____

17. (laf) _____

18. (ˈbe tər) _____

19. (jə ˈraf) _____

20. (ˈjü əl) _____

21. (dīm) _____

22. (rōd) _____

23. (bāk) _____

24. (sēn) _____

25. (fȯl) _____

A dictionary entry gives every definition for a word. Sometimes you will need to read all of the definitions. Then you can find the definition that makes sense in a particular context. The dictionary also gives the part of speech of the word. Most dictionaries use the following short forms of the parts of speech: n. (noun), v. (verb), adj. (adjective), adv. (adverb).

Read the definitions for each word. Then write the number of the definition that makes sense for each sentence.

> **mis sion** (mi ˈshən) *n* **1.** an assigned task **2.** a voyage of a military craft or spacecraft **3.** a group of people sent to represent an organization **4.** a smaller church that is supported by a larger church

1. The mission went to South America to explain our company's offer. _____

2. Our mission was to clean up the park. _____

3. We tracked the space mission on the Internet. _____

> **pose** (pōz) *v* **1.** to present or put forward (a question) **2.** to assume a particular attitude or position in order to be painted, drawn, or photographed **3.** to pretend to be (someone or something) **4.** to behave in a false way in order to impress someone

4. Allen posed as a cook while he was undercover. _____

5. Ping had not thought about how to get home until Chuma posed the question. _____

6. Irakil posed for an hour while the students sketched. _____

> **fair** (fer) *adj* **1.** light or blond **2.** in line with rules or standards **3.** considerable or good enough **4.** beautiful, attractive

7. The umpire made a fair call. _____

8. She is the fairest maiden in the land. _____

9. Natalie had to wear sunblock to protect her fair skin. _____

Circle the answer for each question.

1. Which words are in alphabetical order?

   A beat, beet, beast, beagle

   B beef, beat, beagle, beast

   C beagle, beast, beat, beet

   D beagle, beast, beef, beat

2. The guide words on a page in the dictionary are *mechanic* and *meddle*. Which word would NOT be found on the page?

   F mechanize

   G medal

   H medic

   J medalist

3. The guide words on a page in the dictionary are *reset* and *resist*. Which word would NOT be found on the page?

   A resettle

   B resolve

   C resign

   D resign

4. Which word matches this pronunciation? ('ni kəl)

   F night

   G nickel

   H nick

   J niche

5. Read the dictionary entry below. Which definition makes sense in this sentence?

   She skimmed the fat from the top of the chicken soup after it cooled.

   skim (skim) *v.* **1.** to remove something from the surface of a liquid **2.** to steal or embezzle money **3.** to read quickly to note only the important points **4.** to pass over a surface lightly touching it

   A 1

   B 2

   C 3

   D 4

6. Which word matches this pronunciation? (hed)

   F he'd

   G heard

   H head

   J had

7. Read the dictionary entry below. Which definition makes sense in this sentence?

   The doctor checked my joints during the exam.

   joint (jȯint) *n* **1.** a junction between bones or other parts of the body **2.** a place on a plant stem where a leaf or branch grows **3.** a crack in a rock **4.** (slang) a place or dwelling

   A 1

   B 2

   C 3

   D 4

8. Which word matches this pronunciation? (bak)

   F book

   G bake

   H beak

   J back

9. Which words are in alphabetical order?

   A bread, ball, beard, bill

   B bake, bell, beard, bill

   C beard, bell, bill, bread

   D bake, bread, beard, bell

10. The guide words on a page are *orderly* and *organic*. Which word would be found on the page?

   F ordinary

   G original

   H orchestra

   J orbit

Workplace Skill:
Use a Dictionary When Writing a Résumé

A résumé is a summary of a person's education and work experience. People send their résumés to potential employers when they are looking for a job. It is important to choose the right words in a résumé. It is also important to spell them correctly. A dictionary entry for a word gives all the definitions for the word. You will need to read all of the definitions to find the one that makes sense in a particular sentence.

Résumé

Laurie Paxton   Phone: 262-555-1234
1210 Earl Drive, Newton, WI 88402   lauriepaxton@reachme.net

Education:

Present   Newton Community College
                                   Course of Study: Majoring in English

High School   Baxter High School
                                   Newton, WI
                                   School Band, Soccer Team

Work Experience:

2008–2010   Worked part-time after school as
Newton Daily News   administrative assistant

2007
Fancy Florist   Worked during the summer as a cashier

Laurie Paxton wanted to make sure she was using the word *course* in the correct way in her résumé. She looked up the word in a dictionary, and this is what she found.

---

course (kȯrs) *n* **1.** a forward movement from one point to the next **2.** a way; route; track **3.** a way of acting **4.** an area used for certain sports or games **5.** a series of classes or lessons **6.** a part of a meal served at one time

---

1. What is the meaning of *course* as used in the résumé?

  A a forward movement from one point to the next

  B a way of acting

  C an area used for certain sports or games

  D a series of classes or lessons

2. What does the letter *n* mean after the word *course* in the dictionary entry?

  F It means that the word has several meanings.

  G It tells the part of speech of the word—noun.

  H It tells about the origin of the word.

  J It shows how to pronounce the word.

Write for Work

Using Laurie Paxton's résumé as an example, draft a résumé for yourself. Be sure to include information so that a potential employer will know how to reach you. Write your résumé in a notebook. Use a dictionary to check your spelling and word choices.

Workplace Extension

Assessing the Next Step

Jenny Rodriguez has just graduated from high school. Her friends and relatives keep asking her, "So, what do you want to do now?" Jenny wants to get a job, but she doesn't know what kind of job. She earned good grades in certain classes, especially English. She acquired some experience and skills from summer and after-school jobs, including working at her local newspaper. In addition, Jenny worked as a volunteer writing for the school newspaper. She wonders if she will be able to combine all these things to find a job that's right for her.

Circle the letter the answer to each question.

1. What next step would be most helpful to Jenny in her job search?

    A make a detailed list of her skills and work experiences

    B talk to her best friend about what she has written

    C write a story about high school

    D reread the articles she wrote for the school newspaper

2. Which of the following should Jenny NOT put on a résumé?

    F her academic experience

    G a record of her most recent grades

    H her job at the local newspaper

    J her volunteer work at the school newspaper

Write the answer to the question.

3. Jenny thought about a possible job as a writer. Would her background help her in this kind of a job? Why or why not?

_____

_____

Explore Words

r- CONTROLLED VOWELS

When a vowel is followed by the letter *r*, the vowel stands for a sound that is not short or long. You can hear the *r*-controlled vowel sound in *cart*, *herd*, *shirt*, *more*, and *turn*.

Choose the letter pair that completes each word. Write the letter pair on the lines.

1. Daura's diamond ring really sp_____kles! (or, ar)

2. Monet was a French _____tist. (ur, ar)

3. Do you think this sk_____t fits me well? (ir, or)

4. The runner did not clear the h_____dle. (ur, ar)

CONSONANT PAIRS

The first letter in each of the consonant pairs *wr*, *gn*, and *kn* is silent. The letter *b* in the consonant pair *mb* is silent in one-syllable words. When followed by *e, i,* or *y*, the consonant pair *sc* stands for the sound of *s*.

Write a word from the box next to its definition.

scent	comb	sign	knock	gnaw	wrap

1. to put your name on   _____

2. to chew or nibble   _____

3. to cover a package   _____

4. an odor   _____

5. a tool for styling hair   _____

6. to rap on a door   _____

SPELLING: CONTRACTIONS

A contraction is a short way to write two words. A contraction uses an apostrophe ('). The apostrophe takes the place of letters that are dropped in spoken language. The contraction *didn't* is a shorter way to write or say the words *did not*. The apostrophe takes the place of the letter *o* in *not*.

Write a contraction from the box on the line next to the words it represents.

aren't	isn't	couldn't	you're

1. could not   _____

2. you are   _____

3. is not   _____

4. are not   _____

Reading Basics · Introductory

MULTIPLE-MEANING WORDS

Some words have more than one meaning. For example, the word *shower* can mean "a gentle rain," "to bathe," or "to give generously." You may come across words with multiple meanings as you read. You can use other words in the sentence to figure out which meaning is intended.

Read each sentence. Circle the letter of the answer that gives the meaning of each underlined word.

1. I asked the waiter to bring me a roll and butter.
   a. a small piece of bread
   b. to move by turning over and over

2. Many older adults don't like listening to rock.
   a. a stone
   b. a type of music

3. If the front door sticks, just push it hard.
   a. small twigs
   b. doesn't open

4. It's hard to sleep when it's light outside.
   a. not dark
   b. not heavy

5. This house is well built and very sound.
   a. in good condition
   b. a noise

6. You'll need about a yard of ribbon for the project.
   a. an outdoor area
   b. a measurement equal to three feet

ACADEMIC VOCABULARY

Knowing these high-frequency words will help you in many school subjects.

abbreviate	to shorten a word or phrase
arrange	to put things in a certain order
list	to make a list of
define	to give the meaning of
represent	to stand for something else

Complete the sentences below using one of the words above.

1. I did not have time to _____ the books on my shelves, and now I can't find anything.

2. Tony used a stick figure to _____ each player on the team in his model.

3. Gracia decided to _____ the names of all the employees at the store to make sure she didn't forget anyone.

4. The people at the post office ask that everyone _____ the names of states in the same way when addressing letters.

5. Zaki didn't understand the word, so he couldn't _____ it.

Unit 3 Review

Identify Sequence

The order in which events take place is called sequence. When you read, it is important to understand what happens first, second, and so on. Look for clue words such as *first, next, then,* and *last.* You also need to understand sequence to correctly follow directions.

Compare and Contrast

Comparing shows how two or more things are alike. Contrasting shows how two or more things are different. Writers often compare and contrast in the same passage. Tables can help you compare and contrast information.

Identify Author's Purpose

Authors typically write for one or more of the following purposes: to persuade, to inform, to explain, to entertain, or to describe. To identify an author's purpose, ask yourself questions. For example, have I learned anything from the passage? What have I learned?

Use Graphs

Graphs are a way to show information visually. There are many different kinds of graphs, including line graphs, bar graphs, and circle graphs (also called pie charts). Line graphs and bar graphs are set on axes, using either bars or points and lines to stand for numbers. Circle graphs show percentages as pieces of a "pie."

Read Signs

Signs give information. Some signs have words. Sometimes the shape of a sign is important. Some signs contain symbols. It is important to recognize the symbols and understand what they mean.

Use a Dictionary

Words in the dictionary are arranged in alphabetical order. You can use a dictionary to look up the meaning of a word you don't know. Guide words at the top of each dictionary page help you find the page where the word is. You can also check the spelling and pronunciation of a word in a dictionary.

Unit 3 Assessment

Read each passage. Then circle the letter of the answer to each question.

> The Flyers and the Comets are both good baseball teams. Both teams have great pitchers. Both have been playing in our city for a long time. They have enthusiastic supporters. However, there are differences between the teams. The Flyers are more powerful hitters. They have a solid infield. Also, the Flyers' coach is more experienced. He has coached many of the same players for several years.

1. This passage compares and contrasts
   A two baseball teams.
   B two baseball coaches.
   C two cities.
   D two hitters.

2. How are the Flyers and Comets alike?
   F The teams play on the same field.
   G Both teams have great pitchers.
   H Both teams wear blue uniforms.
   J The teams have the same coach.

> If you are ever shipwrecked in the middle of the ocean, don't drink too much ocean water. Why not? You can die if you drink too much ocean water. An average gallon of ocean water contains more than a quarter pound of salt. The human body needs salt in very small amounts. Drinking a lot of saltwater can dehydrate your body. So, if you ever find yourself lost in the ocean, drink only a small amount of ocean water each day.

3. What is the author's purpose for writing this passage?
   A to entertain readers with a scary story
   B to describe ocean water
   C to explain why people should not drink too much saltwater
   D to tell why the human body needs small amounts of salt

4. Compared to drinking water, ocean water is
   F the same.
   G less salty.
   H much saltier.
   J a little saltier.

5. If you did not know the meaning of the word *dehydrate* in the passage, on which page of the dictionary would you find it?
   A a page with the guide words *degree* and *deity*
   B a page with the guide words *deject* and *delicate*
   C a page with the guide words *delight* and *demand*
   D a page with the guide words *design* and *deter*

The Heimlich maneuver is a way to remove food that is blocking the windpipe. First, stand behind the choking victim. Place your arms around the victim's waist. Make a fist and place it against the victim just below the rib cage. Grasp your fist with your other hand. Press inward and upward with a quick thrust. This action forces air out of the victim's lungs. The air expels the object from the windpipe.

6. What is the first thing you do when performing the Heimlich maneuver?

   F Grasp your fist with your other hand.

   G Place your arms around the victim's waist.

   H Stand behind the victim.

   J Make a fist and place it against the victim's abdomen.

7. What final step results in expelling the object from the windpipe?

   A Place your arms around the victim's waist.

   B Press inward and upward against the abdomen with a quick thrust.

   C Place your fist against the victim's abdomen.

   D Grasp your fist with your other hand.

Read the questions. Then circle the letter of the answer to each question.

8. Which words are in alphabetical order?

   F father, fasten, farewell, fashion

   G raccoon, raffle, radius, random

   H page, pail, pajamas, panel

   J hook, hop, hoop, hope

9. Read the dictionary entry below. Which definition makes sense in this sentence?

The bear retreated when it saw the hikers.

re treat (ri 'trēt) *v* **1.** to move away from danger; withdraw, *n* **2.** a withdrawal of troops **3. a period of quiet and rest 4. a safe place for people and animals**

   A 1

   B 2

   C 3

   D 4

10. If the guide words on a dictionary page are *material* and *maturity*, which word would you NOT be able to find on the page?

   F matter

   G maximum

   H matrix

   J matinee

Study the graphs. Then circle the letter of the answer to each question.

Languages Spoken in the Most Countries

*The numbers reflect countries where the language is spoken. The language is not necessarily the official or dominant language of the country.

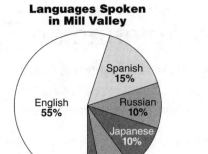

Languages Spoken in Mill Valley

11. Which language is spoken in the most countries?

   A English   **C** Portuguese

   B Arabic   **D** Spanish

12. In Mill Valley, which language is spoken by the fewest people?

   F Russian   **H** Tagalog

   G Spanish   **J** Vietnamese

Circle the letter of the answer that tells what each sign means.

13.

   A pedestrian crossing

   B railroad crossing

   C deer crossing

   D bicycle route

14.

   F bicycle crossing

   G fire lane

   H hospital zone

   J no passing zone

15.

   A no parking

   B signal ahead

   C steep hill

   D do not enter

16.

   F no passing zone

   G no right turn

   H hospital zone

   J no smoking

17.

   A pedestrian crossing

   B bus stop

   C children at play

   D deer crossing

Read the instructions in the box. Then circle the letter of the answer to each question.

Completing an Electronic Time Sheet

In order to make sure your time is recorded at the end of each month, it is important to keep your electronic time sheet up to date. Fill in the information daily if you can, or at the end of each week. Here is a reminder of the steps you need to take:

Step 1: Note the project code of each project you work on. Keep track of the hours you spend on each project.

Step 2: Go to the main page of the internal company website and open the network application TimeCounts.

Step 3: Log in with your employee passcode and click on "Time Sheets."

Step 4: Click on the correct date in the calendar—you need to enter codes for each day individually.

Step 5: Enter each project code and the number of hours you worked on it that day. Your time should add up to eight hours per day.

Step 6: Check your entries carefully and then click on the next date. Repeat the process until you are up to date.

Step 8: Log out of "Time Sheets" and exit the TimeCounts application.

18. What do you do after you click on "Time Sheets"?

    F Open the network application TimeCounts.

    G Log in with your employee passcode.

    H Click on the correct date in the calendar.

    J Go to the main page of the internal company website.

19. What do you do just before you log out of "Time Sheets"?

    A Log in with your employee passcode.

    B Note the project code of the project on which you are currently working.

    C Click on the correct date in the calendar.

    D Make sure you are up to date on the calendar.

20. What is the last step of these instructions?

    F Log in with your employee passcode.

    G Check your entries carefully and then click on the next date.

    H Log out of "Time Sheets" and exit the TimeCounts application.

    J Enter each project code and the number of hours you worked on it.

Read the press release. Then circle the letter of the answer to each question.

Harris Appliances August Newsletter

Milton Hall Reopens Milton Hall will host a grand reopening party at 7 P.M. on Friday, September 19. Harris Appliances will be the main sponsor. We are proud to announce that Letty Anne and the Blue Dog Band will perform. You all know Letty Anne. She is our very own sales manager!

Milton Hall has a brand-new dance floor and a new sound system. The building also has improved fire-safety features. It is now completely handicapped accessible.

Please mark September 19 on your calendars. Bring your neighbors and friends and your dancing shoes! Note that the entrance is the same, but parking is now behind the building.

Refreshments and beverages will be provided by Martha's Catering Company. However, if you would like to bring a special appetizer or dessert, please do! Your delicious homemade treats are always welcome and appreciated.

21. What is the author's purpose in this press release?

   A to tell people that Letty Anne is the sales manager

   B to inform employees about a special event

   C to make a donation to Letty Anne and the Blue Dogs

   D to boast about the new features of Milton Hall

22. If you did not know the meaning of the word *accessible* in the press release, on which page of the dictionary would you find it?

   F a page with the guide words *able* and *accident*

   G a page with the guide words *active* and *actual*

   H a page with the guide words *amber* and *appliances*

   J a page with the guide words *absolute* and *accent*

23. What is one way that Milton Hall is different from what it used to be?

   A It has a smaller dance floor.

   B It has new, remodeled bathrooms.

   C It is completely handicapped accessible.

   D It is much larger.

24. What is one way that Milton Hall is the same as it used to be?

   F It still has an old sound system.

   G The parking lot is in the same place.

   H It still has an old dance floor.

   J The entrance is in the same place.

Circle the letter of the answer to each question.

25. Which word is the plural of *wife*?

  A wifs

  B wifes

  C wivs

  D wives

26. Which word has a long vowel sound in the first syllable?

  F title

  G simple

  H rattle

  J puddle

27. Which word is an antonym of *boring*?

  A interesting

  B tiring

  C dull

  D pounding

28. Which word makes sense in both sentences?

The last note of the song sounded

_____ to me.

The waves have left smooth,

_____ rocks on the beach.

  F wild

  G loud

  H rough

  J flat

29. Which phrase means "the groceries belonging to the Johnsons"?

  A the Johnsons's groceries

  B the Johnsons' groceries

  C the Johnson' groceries

  D the Johnsons groceries

30. Which word has a long *i* sound?

  F thick

  G slip

  H mild

  J chip

31. Which is the correct meaning of *still* in this sentence?

I *still* believe I had the correct answer.

  A continue to

  B not moving

  C previous

  D often

32. Which word has an *r*-controlled vowel?

  F script

  G trolley

  H brand

  J scar

33. Which word correctly completes the sentence?

I know Dave very well, and he is

_____ of cheating on his test.

  A prequalified

  B unsatisfied

  C incapable

  D ungrateful

34. Which word means "can be broken"?

  F unbroken

  G breaker

  H breakable

  J unbreakable

35. Which word is spelled correctly?

  A explodeing

  B reliable

  C thiner

  D flimsyest

36. Which is the correct form of the contraction?

  F is'nt

  G isn't

  H isnt

  J isno't

Posttest

For questions 1–4 circle the letter of the answer that gives the meaning of each sign. For questions 5–8 read the map. Then circle the letter of the answer that best answers the question.

1.

   A poison

   B recycle

   C no smoking

   D exit

2.

   F exit

   G hospital

   H school

   J restaurant

3.

   A no U-turn

   B no right turn

   C divided highway

   D no left turn

4.

   F no bicycles

   G walk

   H signal ahead

   J don't walk

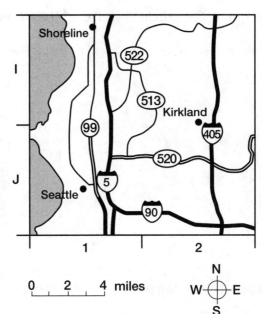

● City or Town   ② State Road

⑨⓿ National Interstate Highway

5. What kind of road is route 5?

   A national interstate highway

   B state highway

   C unpaved road

   D county highway

6. What are the coordinates for Seattle?

   F K2

   G J2

   H J1

   J K3

7. About how far is it from Seattle to Shoreline?

   A 3 miles

   B 9 miles

   C 50 miles

   D 100 miles

8. Which state road is closest to Seattle?

   F 99

   G 513

   H 520

   J 522

Posttest continued

Study the graph. Then circle the letter of the answer to each question.

Favorite Radio Stations

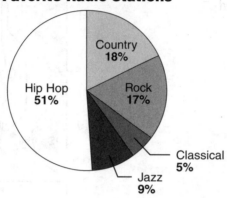

9. What percent of people prefer rock music stations?

   A   5%

   B   9%

   C   17%

   D   18%

10. What kind of radio station do most people prefer?

   F   country

   G   classical

   H   hip hop

   J   jazz

11. Which group of listeners is about half the total?

   A   those who chose jazz

   B   those who chose hip hop

   C   those who chose rock

   D   those who chose classical

12. What kind of radio station is the least favorite?

   F   rock

   G   country

   H   hip hop

   J   classical

Read each passage. Then circle the letter of the answer to each question.

> When Len arrived at the grocery store, it was filled with shoppers. "Oh, no," Len said to himself as he saw the checkout line. "There are four people ahead of me, and each one has a full cart of groceries. I'm going to be here for at least a half hour."
>
> Just then the store manager appeared. "Good morning, sir," he said. "I see you have a small order. Follow me to the express line. I'll have you out of here in a flash."

13. How many people were in line ahead of Len?

   A   half a dozen

   B   four

   C   none

   D   one

14. What character trait does the manager show?

   F   rudeness

   G   laziness

   H   helpfulness

   J   carelessness

When you're calm, your heart beats 60 to 100 times per minute. When you're running or dancing, your heart rate may double. That is because your muscles use more oxygen when you're active. More blood is needed to carry the oxygen. That makes your heart beat faster. All animals have different heart rates. The smaller the animal, the faster the heart rate will be. For example, a hummingbird's heart can beat 1,000 times per minute. An elephant's heart beats 25 times per minute.

15. What causes your heart to beat faster when you're active?

A When you feel better, your heart rate doubles.

B More blood is needed to carry oxygen to your muscles.

C Your muscles need to relax.

D An increased heart rate makes you run faster.

16. A veterinarian is checking a whale's heart rate. About how fast do you predict the heart rate will be?

F 10 times per minute

G 60 times per minute

H 100 times per minute

J 2,000 times per minute

17. From this passage, you can conclude that

A all birds have the same heart rate.

B animals have different heart rates, depending on their size.

C exercise is unhealthy because it doubles your heart rate.

D animals and humans have the same heart rate.

18. When you are sleeping, you heart rate is most likely going to be

F slower than when you are active.

G the same as when you are active.

H about the same as an elephant's.

J about the same as a hummingbird's.

Read the dictionary entry. Then circle the letter of the answer to each question.

live (liv) *v.* **1.** to be alive; **2.** to reside in a particular place; **3.** to spend one's life in a particular way or under particular circumstances

19. In which sentence does *live* use the meaning defined in number 3?

A He lived his whole life in Dublin.

B He lived a long time after his operation.

C They live in fear of an earthquake.

D We lived in a small one-room apartment.

20. Which words are in alphabetical order?

F lift, lingo, list, live

G live, lift, lingo, lame

H lame, list, lingo, live

J lift, list, live, lingo

Posttest continued

Read each passage. Then circle the letter of the answer to each question.

> Proper first aid can save a victim's life. It can also prevent more medical problems. When you see an accident, analyze the situation. Decide whether you can help the victim. If you are unsure, do not attempt treatment. Follow these general steps when giving first aid. First, call for help. Then provide urgent care if the victim is bleeding severely or has stopped breathing. Next, examine the person for other injuries. Finally, wait for help. Do not attempt to do anything you do not know how to do properly.

21. After calling for help, what is the next step in giving first aid?

  A Treat the victim for shock.

  B Examine the victim for additional injuries.

  C Fill out an accident report.

  D Provide urgent care if you know how to do it properly.

22. What is the best paraphrase of the first two sentences of the passage?

  F First aid prevents medical problems.

  G First aid is very important.

  H Everyone should learn how to perform basic first aid.

  J First aid can save lives and prevent additional medical problem.

> Eloisa showed Gerta her closed diary. She told Gerta it was secret. Gerta promised not to read it. When Eloisa left the room, Gerta picked up the diary. She thought about opening it but then quickly put it down. Eloisa returned and saw that the diary was in a different place.
>
> "Did you read my diary?" asked Eloisa.
>
> "I thought about reading it, but I didn't," replied Gerta.

23. Suppose Gerta finds some money on Eloisa's floor. She isn't sure if it belongs to her or to Eloisa. Gerta will probably

  A offer to split the money with Eloisa.

  B say that the money is Eloisa's.

  C tell Eloisa that she found the money.

  D claim that the money is hers.

24. What character trait does Gerta show?

  F selfishness

  G generosity

  H rage

  J honesty

> Emperor penguins can go much longer than humans without food. They are amazing. These penguins have layers of fat that allow them to fast for over two months. They live off their fat reserves during these months. The males incubate the eggs during this time. Most human beings could not go two months without food. Most people need to eat daily. Some people eat three meals a day. Others eat more or less frequently. Some people like to eat small amounts throughout the day. Others think it is healthier to eat a large portion once or twice a day. Almost no one waits two months.

25. What is the main idea of this paragraph?

   A   Both people and penguins eat too much.

   B   Penguins and people store and use food differently.

   C   Fasting is unhealthy.

   D   People have healthier diets than penguins do.

26. Which of these sentences is an opinion?

   F   Almost no one waits two months.

   G   They are amazing.

   H   Most people need to eat daily.

   J   Others eat more or less frequently.

27. What two things are being contrasted?

   A   eating and starving

   B   people and penguins

   C   penguins and other birds

   D   fat and blubber

28. As used in this paragraph, what does the word *fast* mean?

   F   eat a lot quickly

   G   stay in the water

   H   move quickly

   J   go without food

> It is important to eat fruits and vegetables. They have important vitamins. Vitamin C is an important example. For hundreds of years, British sailors got the disease scurvy. They ate only dried meat and bread. Then a doctor found that people who ate citrus fruits did not get scurvy. Starting in 1795, every British Navy ship carried lemon juice. Each day the sailors drank juice. Soon they stopped getting scurvy. Scurvy is caused by a lack of vitamin C. Now, scurvy is usually found only in babies and the elderly. Anyone can get it, though. Eating citrus fruits, tomatoes, and onions keeps it away.

29. What do you think the author's purpose was for writing this passage?

   A   to explain the importance of vitamin C

   B   to describe life on a sailing ship

   C   to persuade readers that citrus is delicious

   D   to describe the taste of lemon juice

30. What caused the sailors to get scurvy?

   F   They ate too much dried meat.

   G   No one knows.

   H   They did not get enough vitamin C.

   J   They caught it from spoiled fish.

Posttest continued

Read the warning label. Then circle the letter of the answer to each question.

> **CLEAN-BURNING WAX**
>
>
>
> **WARNING!**
>
> **To prevent fire:** Burn candle within sight. Keep out of reach of children and pets. Keep away from flammable items. Keep wick trimmed to 1/4 inch to prevent excessive smoke or flame. Do not let debris fall into wax. Discontinue use when only 1/2 inch of wax remains. Never move a hot candle. Never burn near a draft. Never burn unattended.
>
> **Failure to follow instructions could result in fire hazard or injury!**

31. Which of these actions is safe?

   A burn the candle unattended

   B trim the candle's wick

   C burn the candle near a draft

   D move the candle while it is hot

32. What can happen if you do not follow the safety instructions?

   F The candle won't work.

   G You could be injured.

   H Nothing will happen.

   J Debris will get into your candle.

33. How long should the wick be when you are burning the candle?

   A 1/4 inch

   B 1/2 inch

   C 1 inch

   D There is no specified length.

34. When should you stop using the candle?

   F when all the wax has burned

   G when the wick is shorter than 1/4 inch

   H when babies are in the room

   J when 1/2 inch of wax is left

Posttest continued

Read the workplace document excerpt from an employee manual. Then circle the letter of the answer to each question.

Time between Assignments—Bus Drivers

If the time between assignments is 20 minutes or less, drivers will be paid. They will use this time to clean the bus, complete paperwork, or review their trip logs. If drivers need a break longer than 20 minutes, they should take an unpaid break. They may exit the bus and use this time for personal business such as eating or taking a walk.

Telephone Use

All buses are equipped with emergency telephones. Drivers should not use the telephone for personal use or give the phone number to family or friends. Drivers should make calls on the bus phone only when absolutely necessary.

---

35. What is one thing that bus drivers are allowed to do if their time between assignments is 14 minutes?

A take a walk

B sweep the bus

C eat lunch

D not stated

36. What is the best summary of the telephone use section?

F All buses have telephones on them. Drivers shouldn't give the number out or make calls to family or friends while on the route. They can use the phone if it is an emergency.

G Don't give out the number for the bus phone. Drivers can make calls while on the route.

H Drivers should not use the phone on the bus unless it is an emergency.

J Drivers cannot receive calls on the bus phone.

37. What is the main idea of the first section?

A If time between assignments is 20 minutes or less, drivers will keep working, but if it is more, they will take an unpaid break.

B Drivers can use unpaid breaks for personal business.

C Drivers should find a productive use of their time during their breaks.

D Drivers should minimize time between assignments when possible.

38. What do you think the author's purpose was for writing this manual?

F to describe what it is like to be a bus driver

G to persuade people to become bus drivers

H to explain correct procedures for bus drivers to follow

J to explain to bus riders why bus drivers do certain things

Posttest continued

Read the workplace document. Then circle the letter of the answer to each question.

Warehouse Inventory Procedures

At the end of the day, each supervisor will need to make sure that the inventory is accurate for his or her section of the warehouse. This will help the company maintain sufficient supplies to fill all customer orders. It is very important that we do not run out of any items.

There are three sections to be filled out for each item. You will need to list the number of boxes. Then list the number of items in each box. This will be different for each item. Then you will need to multiply the number of boxes by the number of items in each box to get the total. Note any partially full boxes in the margin. Make sure that all shipments have been filled before inventory is taken for the day.

Inventory Form

Angle stop valves   box _____ items per box _____ total _____

Bottle traps   box _____ items per box _____ total _____

Tank lids   box _____ items per box _____ total _____

Globe valves (brass)   box _____ items per box _____ total _____

Oil interceptors   box _____ items per box _____ total _____

---

39. There is one tank lid in each box. If there are seven boxes, what should you write on the "total" line?

   A   1

   B   7

   C   8

   D   nothing

40. As used in the first paragraph, what does the word *sufficient* mean?

   F   too few

   G   plumbing

   H   enough

   J   very heavy

41. How many items are in a box of bottle traps?

   A   1

   B   10

   C   100

   D   not stated

42. Globe valves come in boxes of 10. There is a box with only five valves in it. Where should you note this information?

   F   on the box line

   G   on the items per box line

   H   on the total line

   J   in the margin

43. What needs to be done each day before inventory is taken?

   A   Make sure that the inventory is accurate.

   B   Make sure all three sections on the form are filled out.

   C   Make sure that all shipments have been filled.

   D   Make sure there are no partially full boxes.

44. What is a possible effect of having an inaccurate inventory?

   F   All customer orders may not get filled.

   G   Customers may get more than they ordered.

   H   There will not be room to store supplies.

   J   The warehouse will run out of inventory forms.

Circle the letter of the answer to each question.

45. Which phrase means "the books that belong to Amar"?

   A Amars books

   B Amars book's

   C Amar's books

   D Amars' books

46. Which word has a silent letter?

   F wrap

   G cramp

   H list

   J scamp

47. Which word means "more speedy"?

   A speedyer

   B speedyest

   C speedier

   D speediest

48. Which word has a short vowel sound?

   F cash

   G coach

   H cane

   J clean

49. Which word is a compound word?

   A scented

   B scientific

   C airily

   D aircraft

50. Which word has an *r*-controlled vowel?

   F scram

   G press

   H chart

   J cream

51. Which word is the plural of *baby*?

   A babies

   B babys

   C babes

   D babyes

52. Which phrase means "the cars of the girls"?

   F the girls's cars

   G the girl's cars

   H the girls' cars

   J the girls' cars'

53. Which word means the same or almost the same as the underlined word?

beautiful flower

   A honest

   B pretty

   C ugly

   D sharp

54. Which word fits into both sentences?

Sahila will be late for work if she can't find two shoes that _____.

Karim lit a _____.

   F candle

   G fit

   H lamp

   J match

55. Which word has a long vowel sound in the first syllable?

   A planner

   B paper

   C marker

   D pencil

56. Which word has a hard *g* sound?

   F giant

   G gum

   H gentle

   J manage

57. Which word means "write again"?

   A writeable

   B miswrite

   C unwrite

   D rewrite

58. Which word has a long vowel sound?

    F chimp

    G cram

    H cull

    J cope

59. Which word means the opposite of the underlined word?

    <u>messy</u> room

    A crowded

    B dirty

    C tidy

    D large

60. Which word has a soft *c* sound?

    F canter

    G center

    H count

    J cuff

61. What is the meaning of *misdial*?

    A dial incorrectly

    B dial before

    C dial again

    D dial under

62. Which word means the same or almost the same as the underlined word?

    <u>kind</u> person

    F nasty

    G caring

    H rapid

    J foolish

63. Which word is a compound word?

    A lifting

    B water

    C eyeball

    D calendar

64. Which word fits into both sentences?

    I will _____ a flight for Tuesday.

    Ebo finished reading his _____.

    F hold

    G book

    H reserve

    J novel

65. Which word means the opposite of the underlined word?

    <u>cold</u> day

    A hungry

    B warm

    C famous

    D chilly

66. Which two words are homophones?

    F champ, cramp

    G coin, coil

    H write, right

    J can, cane

67. Which word is a compound word?

    A bookmark

    B cancel

    C reason

    D planters

68. Which is the correct contraction of *they will*.

    F they'll

    G thell

    H the'l

    J they'il

69. In which word does *y* stand for the long *i* sound?

    A jelly

    B reply

    C fancy

    D penny

POSTTEST EVALUATION CHART AND ANSWER KEY

This posttest was designed to check your mastery of the reading skills studied. Use the key on page 200 to check your answers. Then circle the question numbers that you answered incorrectly and review the practice pages covering those skills. Carefully rework those practice pages to be sure you understand those skills.

Tested Skills	Question Numbers	Practice Pages
Recognize and Recall Details	13, 15, 41, 42	14–17
Understand Stated Concepts	35	22–25
Draw Conclusions	17	30–33
Summarize and Paraphrase	22, 36	38–41
Recognize Character Traits	14, 24	46–49
Use Forms	39, 42	54–57
Use Correct Spelling	45, 47, 51, 52, 66, 68	21, 29, 44, 45, 62–65, 85, 93, 100, 117, 125, 148, 165, 172, 173, 180
Find the Main Idea	25, 37	78–81
Identify Cause and Effect	30, 44	86–89
Use Consumer Materials	31–34	94–97
Identify Fact and Opinion	26	102–105
Predict Outcomes	16, 23	110–113
Read Maps	5–8	118–121
Identify Sequence	21, 43	134–137
Compare and Contrast	18, 27	142–145
Identify Author's Purpose	29, 38	150–153
Use Graphs	9–12	158–161
Read Signs	1–4	166–169
Use a Dictionary	19, 20	174–177
Synonyms/Antonyms	53, 59, 62, 65	20, 29, 60, 84, 116, 124, 141
Context Clues	28, 40, 54, 64	37, 53, 69, 108, 140, 181
Phonics/Word Analysis	46, 48, 49, 50, 55, 56, 57, 58, 60, 61, 63, 67, 69	20, 28, 36, 44, 52, 60, 61, 68, 84, 92, 100, 101, 108, 109, 116, 124, 140, 148, 149, 156, 157, 164, 172, 180

	KEY		
1.	B	38.	H
2.	G	39.	B
3.	A	40.	H
4.	J	41.	D
5.	A	42.	J
6.	H	43.	C
7.	B	44.	F
8.	F	45.	C
9.	C	46.	F
10.	H	47.	C
11.	B	48.	F
12.	J	49.	D
13.	B	50.	H
14.	H	51.	A
15.	B	52.	H
16.	F	53.	B
17.	B	54.	J
18.	F	55.	B
19.	C	56.	G
20.	F	57.	D
21.	D	58.	J
22.	J	59.	C
23.	C	60.	G
24.	J	61.	A
25.	B	62.	G
26.	G	63.	C
27.	B	64.	G
28.	J	65.	B
29.	A	66.	H
30.	H	67.	A
31.	B	68.	F
32.	G	69.	B
33.	A		
34.	J		
35.	B		
36.	H		
37.	A		